A Contemplative Mystic

Marie Gundersen

A Contemplative Mystic

First published in Australia by Marie Gundersen 2019

Copyright © Marie Gundersen 2019
All Rights Reserved

 A catalogue record for this book is available from the National Library of Australia

ISBN: 978-0-646-80940-3 (pbk)

Typesetting and design by Publicious Book Publishing
Published in collaboration with Publicious Book Publishing
www.publicious.com.au

No part of this book may be reproduced in any form, by photocopying or by any electronic or mechanical means, including information storage or retrieval systems, without permission in writing from both the copyright owner and the publisher of this book.

Contents

Acknowledgments	i
Introduction	iii
Chapter 1: Background	1
Chapter 2: Norway	5
Chapter 3: Australia	11
Postscript	97
Reflections on the Journey	99
Divine Law	115
Appendix A: Correspondence	119
Appendix B: "St. John of the Cross and the Dark Night of the Soul"	127
Timeline of Mystical Experiences	135
Selected Bibliography	137

Acknowledgments

Without Divine guidance, this book would not have been written.

I had never felt the need to write a diary until my first mystical experience in 1973. From that time on, I recorded all my unusual experiences as well as my process of spiritual transformation. This book is based on my diaries.

When I joined the Spiritual Emergence Network of Australia (SEN Australia) in 1998, I met the coordinator, Gini Witt, who was also the editor of the SEN journal *Emergence*. At the time we were both living in Lismore, New South Wales. Thanks to Gini's encouragement and skilful editing, I wrote two articles for *Emergence*. Years later, these articles were pivotal in making a connection with Father Thomas Keating. Thanks to his suggestion and encouragement, I was inspired to write a book.

Father Thomas Keating (1923–2018) was a former Abbot of St. Joseph's Abbey in Spencer, Massachusetts, and a Cistercian monk and priest of St. Benedict's Monastery in Snowmass, Colorado. He was the founder of the Centering Prayer Movement and of Contemplative Outreach.

When I returned to Lismore (after living in another part of Australia for twelve years), Gini was there and agreed to help with the editing. She recognised the need for a narrative to make the book more engaging for the reader. We had long conversations in which I learned to articulate my experiences, and Gini gained a deeper understanding of the journey of a contemplative mystic. It was very helpful that she is such a good listener and has a background in counselling psychology.

I am deeply humbled by and grateful for Father Thomas Keating's support through prayers and correspondence and to Gini who has shown an unwavering commitment to this book project—a dedication that can best be described as divinely inspired.

Introduction

In 1973, I had an extraordinary encounter in an office building in Oslo. Waiting for me in the lift was a stranger wearing a dark robe and carrying a large bundle of keys. This meeting heralded the beginning of a series of mystical experiences and a process of spiritual transformation.

Two years later, as I stepped across the threshold to my bedroom, I experienced an inner calling. I made a vow to serve God. From that moment on, my life had meaning and purpose. Who had called me and where I was going I did not know—but I had a sense that I would be guided.

In 1977 I left Norway, the country of my birth, and came to live in Australia with Patrick, my four-year-old son. The decision to leave family and everything familiar was informed by an inner knowing that this was meant to be. We settled in the Adelaide Hills close to where a new Rudolf Steiner school was being established. Our involvements with the school and the local community soon forged new friendships.

I remember thinking one day: 'It is not possible to be happier than this. What now?'

Soon after, I was given a book on meditation by J. Krishnamurti, *Freedom from the Known*. After reading this book, I felt inspired to start meditating. This was in 1982. Over time, meditation led to increased self-awareness, the healing of emotional wounds and the erasing of conditioning. I continued to have mystical experiences. Why these were happening to me and what they meant I did not know, but I wrote them down in the hope that one day all would be revealed.

My life changed dramatically in 1990. I woke up one night with a spinning sensation in the head. A tremendous force entered my body, making it feel like a completely hollow space. A profound change of consciousness had happened—the observer and the observed had merged! Any inward looking or attempt to move out of this state was impossible; self-reflection and emotional feedback had ceased. Whenever I tried to describe to others what it was like to live in the Now and in a body where there is 'no one home,' it made no sense to them. Outwardly I appeared my usual self, energetic and positive, but inside I felt exiled and unable to re-enter the old familiar world. I kept on journaling, detailing the effects of this cataclysmic shift, while continuing to focus on family life.

I searched for answers in spiritual literature but found that the teachings of Buddhism and Christianity tended to focus on the actual practices rather than describing what can occur as a result of these practices.

Discovering the teaching of St. John of the Cross was a Godsend. This sixteenth-century Spanish mystic writes on what he calls the 'Dark Night of the Soul.' He describes feelings of emptiness and annihilation as a stage towards union with God. This gave me hope for a positive outcome.

In 1999, again during the night, a powerful force ascended through my body and released me from the 'tomb' of confinement into a state of Pure Awareness. The vessel had been hollowed out in 1990, and after a 'gestation period' of nine years, a channel had been opened for the inflow of Divine Light. From darkness into light—a new stage and a new state of being. The outcome of this 'rebirth' in 1999 was a profound state of inner peace—a peace that is not of this world and cannot be reflected on.

Increasingly, I had become aware that the expression the 'Dark Night of the Soul' was being used to describe an emotional/mental experience of depression. St. John of the Cross says: '… nothing worldly satisfies one who has tasted the Divine.' This is not a psychological need but a spiritual need.

The misinterpretation of St. John of the Cross's teaching prompted me to write. I was concerned that spiritual seekers enduring the 'Dark Night of the Soul' would have difficulty finding spiritual guidance and risk being pathologised. I wrote the articles *A Modern Mystic* (based on my own spiritual journey) and *St. John of the Cross and the Dark Night of the Soul*, which were published 2007 in *Emergence* (the journal of SEN Australia.)

Having discovered the contemplative dimension of Christianity, I started reading Father Thomas Keating's books. Feeling attuned to his teachings, I wrote to thank him for his invaluable contributions to the contemplative life and included the SEN journal issue with my two articles.

Father Thomas Keating's reply was most unexpected! He encouraged me to enlarge on these two articles and write a book. This was a real blessing. I felt validated, and this in turn motivated me to sort through my old handwritten diaries and save them on a computer.

I had not looked at these notes until I started transcribing them. Only then did I notice that there were recurring symbols linking all the different mystical experiences and references to scripture.

This posed the question: Is there a message here for the world and not just for me?

1
Background

I was born close to midnight on 20 December 1946 in Oslo, Norway, and I was baptised in the Lutheran Church as Aase Marie Gundersen. I lived with my parents and only brother in an apartment block in Oslo until I was sixteen. My mother was a stay-at-home mum, saintly in her kindness and capacity for self-sacrifice. She was naturally mindful, focussing on whatever she was doing and never engaging in gossip. She had a gift for writing poetry. I adored her.

My father excelled in business. He was intellectually brilliant but emotionally unavailable. The relationship between my parents was strained and lacked affection and intimacy. I looked up to my brother who was six years older than me, and I knew I could rely on him for support and guidance. He teased me a lot, but we never quarrelled.

My earliest recollection of what may be termed an unusual 'activity' was lying in bed before I went to sleep imagining I was flying. By running fast I could take off—and with a vigorous swimming motion—'fly' a short distance. These were not out-of-body experiences but felt very real. During these nightly 'flights,' I was called the 'great Aase' and the 'ordinary

Aase.' The 'great one' could fly, but as soon as she landed, she was 'the ordinary' Aase again.

My maternal grandmother taught me to pray when I was a very young child. Each night before going to sleep, I would recite the two prayers she had taught me: the Lord's Prayer (in Norwegian) and another, shorter prayer thanking Jesus for all the good things that had happened to me that day. There were times when it was hard to find something good to be grateful for. This little prayer taught me to look for moments of grace even in the midst of sorrow—it could always be worse.

As a young child I used to ponder the concept of infinity and kept asking my father what was beyond the stars. Space needed to end somewhere, I thought. My mind tried to grasp what would be behind the next star and so on. In the end, I settled for infinity as endless space. A circle or ring, I remember telling my father, was like infinity—something that has no visible beginning or end.

Periodically throughout childhood, I developed very high fevers with no other symptoms of infection. This was not treated as anything unusual.

I loved playing games with friends and was far too busy with after-school activities to focus much on homework. During primary school I enjoyed ballet, gymnastics, ballroom dancing, Girl Guides, craft classes, school choir, hiking, skiing, skating and swimming. I used to run up and down the seventy-two steps to our apartment many times a day. The backyards behind the apartment blocks were havens for interactive games for children of all ages. In the winter there was enough snow to construct igloos where secret club meetings were held, lit up inside by candlelight.

When I was in primary school, my brother suggested I stop reading *Miss Detective* books and check out our father's bookshelves for better literature. Thanks to him, I discovered that leather-bound books without pictures were not boring. After reading a series of Jack London's adventure books, I found a book by Lin Yutang that inspired an interest in philosophy.

Our main teacher through primary school made learning interesting and relevant. At an early age she instilled in us the value of honesty and fairness. She was a great role model, and we all loved her. On our yearly report cards we were assessed, not only for the different subjects we had studied, but also for behaviour and presentation. Halfway through primary school, our teacher went to America for six months and we had a relief teacher.

One day during a lesson, a student made a funny comment, and I was the first to burst out laughing. The teacher reacted quickly and sternly told me to leave the class. Being sent home for misbehaving had never happened in our class before. I felt as if I had committed a crime and was deeply ashamed. This incident was not discussed afterwards, and it took me years to understand the reason why the teacher had reacted this way. I did not realise at the time that we had a student in our class with special needs. The relief teacher must have thought we were making fun of this student's disability. The shame I felt was devastating. I was unable to make a sound whenever I felt like laughing for the next twenty-five years! Spiritually I am sure there was a positive side to this trauma, which made me less outgoing and more inward-looking.

I married my first boyfriend when I was twenty and had my first child, Mikkel, when I was twenty-three while living in Australia. Two years later we separated. Due to a set of extraordinary circumstances, deceit and legal mishandling around the custody of our child, I lost contact with Mikkel. I felt like my son had been abducted, and the pain was excruciating. The separation from and loss of my first child turned a page on 'the book of life': a new chapter had started.

The next man to enter my life introduced me to a whole new way of looking at the world. He was well-read and opened my mind to exploring human behaviour through a wide lens of philosophy, psychology (in particular Jungian psychology) and metaphysical science. We first met in Australia, and later he came to live with me in Oslo where we both worked for the same company. It was in this office building that something extraordinary happened one day.

2
Norway

1973: August

I was working for a company in Kristian August's gate in Oslo ('gate' means street in Norwegian). My office was in the computer department on the ground floor. For security reasons, all employees had their own key to unlock the lift doors at the floors occupied by our company. Other businesses were leasing offices on floors unlocked and open to the public. The eight women in my office usually went to lunch together.

On this particular day, I was the last to catch the lift to our canteen, which was on the top floor. As soon as I opened the office door to the corridor and stairwell, I noticed that the door of one of the two lifts was half open. I saw no one else in the corridor at the time, and the opened door seemed to indicate that someone was already waiting (for me?) in the lift. From that moment onwards, my mind went blank, which is something I only realised when the whole experience was recalled later on.

I walked past the person in the lift and stood behind him. I noticed he was carrying a large soft drink bottle and a big bundle of keys. He was obviously going for lunch, I thought, and the keys suggested he was working for us. I pressed the button and the two of us (or should I say three, because I was pregnant at the time) travelled from the ground floor to the seventh floor. Nothing was said between us. I remember noticing that he was wearing a long dark robe and was of medium height with black hair covering his neck (unusual in those days). I did not see his face, but somehow I knew he was an East Asian or Middle Eastern person. When we reached the top floor, out of a sense of courtesy, I unlocked the door with my own key. When I left the lift, he did not. I heard the door close behind me and the lift descending. I walked to the canteen and joined the others for lunch as if nothing unusual had happened.

This unusual experience was completely 'forgotten' until the following night when I was reading a book about various metaphysical and unexplained phenomena. In one chapter there was a comment that worldwide, there had been reports of individuals encountering a man dressed in black with Asian features—supposedly an extraterrestrial making contact! Suddenly my memory was triggered, and I remembered the experience in the lift in vivid detail. I felt a mixture of amazement and fear and wondered what it all meant. That night I dreamt my newborn baby was sitting on the floor making adult conversation. (Patrick was born in October 1973.)

The fact that my memory and rational mind had been altered during the time I was in the lift caused me concern. This had never happened to me before. In my ordinary state of mind, I would have wondered who this person was and asked him which office he worked in. His appearance would have seemed very strange to me, more so because in those days there were very few foreigners living in Norway. The oversized drink bottle and large number of keys would also have seemed odd. I made inquiries at work about this person, but no one else had seen him or knew anything about him. I only shared the mysterious dimension of this experience with Patrick's father, who accepted my story.

1975: February

I was travelling home alone one night after attending a Theosophical Society meeting in Oslo. To get back to my village from the station, I had to walk across snow-covered fields on a narrow path lit by lamp posts. It was very cold, and the compacted snow under my feet made a squeaky sound as I walked along. It had stopped snowing, and there was a lot of fresh snow on the ground.

I saw two guys in the distance walking ahead of me on the only path across the fields to the village. It was late at night, and there were no other people or houses in sight, which made me feel a little uneasy. I glanced up at the starlit night sky, wondering if maybe we are looked after... just a fleeting thought. Shortly afterwards, I became aware of a person on my left, almost touching me as he passed. He walked at the same pace about one metre ahead of me. As we were walking along the path, I realised that my companion's footsteps were silent while mine were still making the usual squeaky sound. Just as I was starting to think this was strange, we passed one of the lamp posts, and under the bright light this person suddenly vanished into thin air! I looked at the soft and untouched snow on both sides of the path and could see no footprints anywhere. I suddenly had the irrational thought that what I had seen was my own shadow. I thought no more of it; in the distance, I could now see the village and felt safe for the rest of the walk home.

It was not until I put the key in my front door that I realised how bizarre this experience had been. In my usual state of mind, I would have exchanged a few words with the person who passed me and would have been startled by his sudden disappearance. Remembering how I had been comforted by the presence of the stranger made me wonder if my little 'prayer' for protection had been answered. I also reflected on the fact that my mind and reasoning had been altered: this had only happened once before, during the mysterious encounter in the lift in 1973.

1975: May

As I stepped across the threshold to my bedroom one day, I experienced an inner calling. I made a vow to serve 'God.' From that moment on, my life had meaning and purpose. Who had called me and where I was going I did not know, but I had a sense that I would be guided.

1976: February

By the time Patrick was three, it was clear that he had a natural talent for drawing and painting and was even drawing three-dimensional pictures. He enjoyed the company of children older than himself who were more focussed on their tasks than children his own age. For a few hours each week, he joined in with activities at the local preschool. While he was there, I spent the time in the library researching different religions and spiritual practices.

I used to take Patrick home from preschool on my bicycle. On this particular day, the road was covered in snow (nothing unusual for Norway). I was focussed on cycling in the track made by the wheels of the vehicle ahead when I happened to look up. The clouds parted, and there appeared a clearly outlined cross in the sky. Somehow I understood that the vision was just for me, so I didn't stop to share this experience with anyone nearby. What went through my mind was that the cross could be a symbol of matter and spirit intersecting in the centre.

I never doubted what I saw. I thought the timing was interesting: that the vision of the cross was related to what I was researching. The previous year, I had officially left the Lutheran Church—the state Church of Norway. Whilst going to church had seemed irrelevant to me, I had continued saying the prayers my grandmother had taught me. It was an important ritual for me to recite the Lord's Prayer with folded hands before going to sleep.

My husband was an Australian citizen and had always wanted our son to grow up in Australia. He thought the multicultural environment would be an advantage. When Patrick was three, we sold our house in preparation for the move to Australia. There were some unforeseen circumstances, and it was decided that Patrick and I should leave first while my permanent resident's visa was still valid. (The plan was for Patrick's father to follow us to Australia as soon as possible, but because he had met another woman, it was years before he relocated to Australia. For a brief couple of years, Patrick enjoyed close contact with his dad before he tragically died of a heart attack.)

3
Australia

1977: November

Realising we would arrive in Australia not knowing anybody, I had placed a notice seeking penfriends in the *Adelaide Advertiser*. I felt it would be important to make connections with other families in advance. When we arrived in Adelaide, Patrick and I were met by Frank, an elderly, Irish, family man who was one of these correspondents. He was very helpful and protective of us, and we ended up renting a house in the Adelaide Hills close to where he lived.

Eden Hills

1978: April

A visitor to my home seemed to be interested in unusual phenomena, so I decided I would mention my experience in the lift in Oslo. As soon as I started describing it to him, we both heard a loud noise. Although it was a still day, a very strong wind made the windows vibrate—we were both startled. I stopped talking, and the wind ceased as suddenly as it had started! This extraordinary experience validated for me the mysterious nature of the meeting in the lift. And whoever he was—he was still around! It was unsettling to know that this being had the power to appear and disappear and knew what I was thinking. I was left wondering why this was happening to me and what it all meant.

1979: February

My mother, aged seventy and not speaking a word of English, travelled alone all the way from Norway to visit us. It was lovely to see her again, and we enjoyed her company for a couple of months. Patrick, who was bilingual by then, interacted with his grandmother through games and storytelling. My mother had a bad back and had suffered from sciatica for many years. I took her for acupuncture treatments in Adelaide, and this really helped her. Over the years, Patrick and I went back to Norway for holidays paid for by my parents.

Littlehampton

1979: November

Patrick and I moved to a little town in the Adelaide Hills close to where the new Rudolf Steiner school was being established. A charming, old, stone cottage, purchased cheaply due to a leaking roof and salt damp, became our much-loved home. I enjoyed the creativity of renovating the cottage and establishing a garden. Life was good; activities were child-oriented. Our involvement with the school and the local community soon forged new friendships.

Every night I used to recite a little prayer I had made up for Patrick. If I forgot, he would remind me to say this: 'May the Good Light shine over us and inside us—and bring peace, happiness, good health and good dreams. Thank you.'

1980: November

One night I awoke, and in the dark I saw a spiritual being sitting at the end of my bed. Looking at him, I noted he had dark, wavy, shoulder-length hair. He touched my big toe and stretched it into a cone shape. I could see this but did not feel anything. When I looked at him again, I could see streams of pale blue, white and pink light around his head. This was the first time I had seen an aura, and I was surprised it had colours. As if he had read my thoughts, the colours around his head changed into a golden glow that looked like the haloes I was familiar with from religious pictures. He then vanished. I was wide awake; I knew this was neither a dream nor something I had imagined. I reflected on the fact that not only was he clearly visible in the pitch-dark room, but even without my glasses, I had seen everything in detail as if I had been wearing them (I am very short-sighted).

1981: March

I was woken up in the middle of the night by three eerie bird calls. The notes were loud and clear, but I knew this was not a real bird. There was an unusual quietness in the room after these calls, and I felt a mixture of anticipation and anxiety. Lying in bed on my right side, I suddenly noticed that something was happening behind me. I could feel a strong force coming out through my back and heard the flapping of the bedclothes. Too scared to turn over, I managed to put my left hand behind my back and felt what seemed like a long, soft 'spine' with bony joints separated from my body! The next thing I knew, I was in my parents' flat in Oslo 'flying' from room to room and turning on all the light switches. I was surprised that I remembered exactly where all the switches were. My father was sitting in the lounge room and did not notice me. I had wanted to tell him something. Then my brother walked into the room and I told him that **'Fear is overcome only when it is experienced to its very limits.'**

After this message had been delivered, I found myself travelling through a dark 'tunnel' where I watched some sheep peacefully grazing while 'on fire'—their bodies looked red hot! I was amazed at their serenity. Suddenly I was back in my bed in Littlehampton. I felt totally relaxed and at ease, which seemed unusual after such an extraordinary ordeal. I then went back to sleep. The whole experience, including the message for my brother, seemed very strange. I checked with my brother who said he had no recollection of our meeting or of any lights being turned on that day.

1981: May

Patrick (now seven years old) woke me up insisting he wanted to sleep in my bed, which was unusual. He quickly went back to sleep. I then felt the anticipation that I had learned to associate with something mysterious being about to happen.

Suddenly I heard a loud roar and could feel a tremendous force, which was somehow not separate from me—it resembled a jumbo jet about to take off. At that moment, I began praying for Divine protection: 'Please, whatever happens, may it be for a good purpose.' I could feel this awesome force increasing, and the sound of the roar grew louder. When it peaked, I was suddenly catapulted into space! There was no sensation of motion, but where I ended up seemed far, far away.

My one and only concern was that Patrick needed me. The moment I thought of him, I was back in my body with a jolt and a noise, which sounded like smashing glass! Soon afterwards, this same force started to rev up, and again I was projected into space. I knew what had worked last time, so I 'willed' myself back and sat up in bed to prevent another 'trip.' Fortunately, Patrick slept through it all. There were no physical side effects from these out-of-body experiences.

1981: 9, 10, 11 June

Tuesday: I had a severe headache and stomach pain.
Wednesday: I stopped eating and had a fever of 40 °C.
Thursday: I experienced a sensation of compression in my solar plexus. In the evening, my fever reduced to 37.5 °C, and I was feeling a lot better. I had not taken any medication for my 'illness.'

During that night (11–12 June), I woke up and witnessed another reality: I was seeing the letters EMAD. I realised that these letters read back to front spelled DAME and that this word meant the same in English and Norwegian. I was given to understand that this word was directed to me and entitled me to enter. Just then, a strong force and sound built up, which I could both hear and feel inside me. This force thrust me into a large unlit space, which seemed to be a great hall. I was overawed and, faced with this unknown reality, I placed all my trust in the Divine power, uttering: 'God help me!'

I found myself on my back on what seemed to be a large, flat, stone slab. I was entirely alone. Suddenly, a dragon-like monster was on top of me and a big claw-like hand was pressing down on my chest. I was terrified but managed to control my emotions. I knew that unless the weight of the dragon's hand lifted, I would suffocate. As soon as I wished for that to happen, the dragon lifted off me. I realised I could control the movement of the dragon with my will. I then watched myself walk out of the hall with the dragon bundled under my arm. The dragon had been conquered! In a flash, I was back in my bed at home.

I knew without doubt that this had not been a dream. I checked my temperature after this fearful ordeal and found it to be normal. I felt relaxed and soon went to sleep. Reading the newspaper the next day, I was surprised to see the Queen's Honours List of Knights and Dames!

For some time I had been aware of a pearl-sized blue light in the periphery of my vision. I noticed that this unusual light phenomenon had disappeared.

1981: 7 October

A vivid dream: I am watching two full moons in the sky. The one to the left is moving slowly towards the other. I panic, telling myself to wake up so I can check if this is really happening. Two moons colliding—catastrophe! Instead of waking up, I watch as the scene unfolds. The moon to the left, with sharper and clearer features, slides across the old, real moon. Fortunately, no collision. The 'new' moon, which looks like a disc, covers the old moon—one precisely behind the other. The surface of this 'new configuration' features an image of a goose. I wake up thinking about Mother Goose and the story of 'The Princess and the Golden Goose.'

Years later, I found a reference to two moons in George Gurdjieff's writing where he talks about 'freeing ourselves from the influence of the Moon by creating a second Moon—a permanent centre of gravity within ourselves.' Was this relevant to my dream?

The loss of Mikkel, my first child, had been a traumatic experience that affected me deeply. Eventually, when the energy of loss and grief had 'run its course,' I found that I had a deeper capacity for love, which found expression in caring for other children as well as my own. (I worked as an assistant in a Steiner preschool and also looked after children in my own home.) Despite the ongoing sadness of losing Mikkel, the depth of despair had been transformed into a more expanded state of joy.

Joan Carter, a psychic and editor of the journal *Phoenix*, once said to me: 'There are two kinds of people—the Givers and the Takers. Givers have to be careful not to let Takers become Grabbers.' These words stayed with me. During a psychic reading, she also told me I would be writing in the future—which seemed odd to me at the time.

Joan knew of my work and engagement with children and suggested I write an article about childhood. *The Way of the Child* was published in *Phoenix* in 1982. Here is an extract:

THE WAY OF THE CHILD

A young child is not engaged in comprehending the world intellectually, but in experiencing it. When a child is absorbed in something, maybe enjoying the beauty of a flower, or following the silver trail of a snail, or absorbed in the sound of drizzling rain, talking to the child interferes and breaks that magic moment of wonder. Interference may not necessarily only be adult talk (which although well meant, is often an untimely lecturing with adult concepts), but it may also be the breaking up of the day with moves from place to place, so that one activity follows another in a collection of disjointed events. This may well be a major cause of the hyperactivity and lack of concentration which is common in children today. Just as there are seasonal changes in nature so does a child need both activity and quiet; times to experience and times to digest these experiences.

If the intellect, the centre of thinking and reasoning, is active all the time, other areas of perception become passive, and we become unbalanced. True teaching must awaken feelings such as wonder, reverence, awe, patience, humility, gratitude and devotion.

In a kindergarten, I often observed that, after listening to a genuine fairy tale, the children's faces looked smooth and peaceful, as after a good night's sleep. The importance of fairy tales and legends lies in the fact that, when told with involvement and understanding of the content, they enable the children to feel the essence of the story with their whole being.

… From one piece of paper a number of pieces can be cut, which can be counted. This simple demonstration will delight children and give them the feeling that parts derive from the whole.

1982

Early in January, I took Patrick with me interstate on a 'Renewal of the Dreamtime' camp. This wilderness camp was an opportunity for us to learn something about the Aboriginal way of life. Every morning we woke up to the sounds of clap sticks and in the dark followed an Aboriginal elder to the top of a hill to watch the sun rise. We were not accustomed to bathing naked nor listening to stories while sitting in a cave on a sacred mountaintop. In many ways, this was a life-changing experience.

While we were away, Paul—a friend of a friend—was house-sitting our cottage. This is how we met. On my return from the camp, I knew instantly that we were 'destined' for each other. This surprised me as I had been happy and fulfilled as a single parent and was not looking for another relationship. It was Paul who introduced me to the teaching of Jiddu Krishnamurti. Paul was involved with the Krishnamurti Information Centre in Adelaide where they showed videos of Krishnamurti's public talks.

Krishnamurti talks about the need to become aware of all our conditioning and to see that our likes, dislikes and opinions are determined by this conditioning. Giving each moment our full attention, is what Krishnamurti calls meditation. It has no beginning and no end; meditation is not something done outside the conditions of everyday life.

Some of my friends were doing sitting meditation as a daily practice. I had tried meditating once, sitting erect and cross-legged—very soon I experienced a rush of energy to the head that produced a heightened state of bliss. This wasn't so different to how I normally felt. I had no inclination to repeat this exercise. Being an active person, Krishnamurti's approach to meditation appealed to me. Instead of sitting cross-legged and meditating at set times, I observed my thoughts, feelings and actions while I was engaged in daily activities. I soon became aware that tasks were done while I was mentally elsewhere—that was a real insight. Awareness from moment to moment was a very demanding form of meditation, but I knew I needed to do it.

1982: April

Not long after Paul had moved in with us, I decided to tell him about the stranger I had encountered in the lift in Oslo. We were sitting in the kitchen, and I had just started to describe this when we both heard three knocks on the front door. We went straight to the door and opened it—no one was there! This reminded me that once before when I started talking about 'the man in the lift,' I had been interrupted by a sudden strong 'wind.' Was I not meant to talk about him? Or maybe it was important that I had a witness?

1984

Patrick had been corresponding with a Tibetan boy while he was in primary school. This was a connection we had made through an Australian teacher who worked in a school for Tibetan children in northern India. She had sent us some Tibetan prayer mats, which I was going to try and sell in a Community Aid Abroad shop in Adelaide. The profit from the sale of these mats was going back to the teacher's school and the community there. When one of the mats didn't sell, I decided to buy it so I could pay them for all their mats. They were all handwoven, square, carpet mats. The one I bought had no obvious image on it. The other mats, which depicted a mandala, had sold quickly.

Our Tibetan prayer mat was very special to us, and we hung it on the wall in the lounge room so that we could enjoy the bright colours. After some time, I took the mat down to give it a clean and realised that it had been hanging upside down. Suddenly I saw a dragon with a large white claw. This claw looked like a hand and immediately brought back my out-of-body experience with the dragon that had tried to crush me! [photo 1]

1986: December

It was time to sell the little fairy-tale cottage in Littlehampton. This had been a much-loved home during Patrick's primary school years, but now it was too small for the three of us. I found it emotionally hard to move on, yet it felt right to do so.

We bought a sixty-acre, sheep-grazing property in Kanmantoo. Paul and I started building a cottage there while we rented in Hahndorf, another town in the Adelaide Hills.

We were inexperienced, and it was hard work building without power tools, but that is what we did! Patrick continued his education at the same Steiner school as before. Friends liked visiting us and sometimes camped on site. The children enjoyed skateboarding down the hills and looking for garnets in the creek. In terms of living there permanently, we agreed with our friends that the remoteness and lack of services would be challenging. [photos 3-8]

Hahndorf

1987: August

One day I was told by an inner voice: 'You will be turned inside out.' This message was repeated a few times during the next couple of weeks. The voice was not coming from my mind, and the message did not mean anything to me. Then one morning when I woke up, my body was in a state of shock. From then on, I experienced rapid heart palpitations and fear day and night lasting about ten seconds, then no symptoms for about the same time, then on again. The symptoms were not thought-related and felt like a physical phenomenon over which I had no control. I felt 'open' with no protection from external impressions. Being in traffic felt like a roller-coaster ride, so I had to stop driving. I had a checkup with a heart specialist who found nothing wrong. Out of desperation, I discovered a way to short-circuit the anxiety attacks by breathing in quickly and at the same time, focussing my attention on my forehead. I was in this state for over two years, day and night.

During this time, I had so much physical energy that I was able to haul rocks dug up from around our property to the site where we were building a cottage. I also planted hundreds of trees and carted buckets for watering. My GP would have liked to prescribe Valium, but personally I wonder whether all the physical exertion might have saved my life. Eventually I found a Chinese doctor who gave me a series of acupuncture treatments for the palpitations, and over time the anxiety attacks became more sporadic. I also saw a homoeopath who gave me remedies for what he described as a perforated sympathetic nervous system.

One day I noticed a tickling below the left ear and brushed off what turned out to be a big black spider. A couple of days later, driving through town, I suddenly felt a tickling under the right ear this time and brushed off a grey Huntsman spider! Surprisingly, I did not panic. (I have always found spiders creepy and used to experience nightmares after I came to live in Australia, dreaming that a large spider crawled on my skin— something that until now had never actually happened. In Norway, I knew of only one spider, and that was the spindly daddy-long-legs!) The spiders left me with no symptoms or marks on my skin. Some time after the encounters with the spiders, I started to notice a 'stiffness' down both sides of my neck. From 1987 onwards, I was aware of heat spots the size of twenty-cent coins moving from the toes up to the head. By 1990, these heat spots had increased in size and were more like patches of heat flaring up momentarily, mainly on my face and head. Palpitations were rare, but headaches had become a problem. Sometimes I experienced a piercing pain through what felt like a crack in the centre of the skull. A chronic sore lump developed on the right side of the nape of the neck, which swelled up during these headaches. After I began chiropractic treatments for my neck, the pain eased and the lump disappeared.

Discovering Gopi Krishna's book on Kundalini was very helpful as it was the first time I had come across a description of the effects of Kundalini as well as the link with meditation. I now wondered if my symptoms had something to do with my meditation practice—even though our experiences were not identical.

> *I did not know then what I came to grasp later on—that an automatic mechanism, forced by the practice of meditation, had suddenly started to function with the object of reshaping my mind to make it fit for the expression of a more heightened and extended consciousness, by means of biological processes as natural and as governed by inviolable laws as the evolution of species or the development and birth of a child.*
> —Kundalini: Evolutionary Energy in Man
> by Gopi Krishna

1990: 6 June

Copy of Paul's handwritten account:

> *An incident which occurred in the early hours of the morning approx. 4 am. I was relating the story of a science fiction film I had seen to Marie. I had seen this film while she was in Norway and was*

struck by the coincidence—that is an alien in a lift with a woman.

The message in the film was of a space man coming to Earth with a warning of global destruction unless mankind ceased its endless violence. Violence which could affect other worlds due to atomic warfare. It was this message the alien wished to give world leaders at one meeting. However even getting all leaders together in one place (Washington) was impossible as they would not agree on the location of the meeting. For this reason the now hunted alien designed a plan to convince world leaders of his power and capabilities. At a set time all power over the Earth would stop. Hence the scene in the film of the lift stopping for ½ hour with alien and friendly landlady aboard. This of course reminded me of Marie's story of years ago; the encounter with a bizarre character in a lift in Norway. A meeting which has become of great significance to her and to which she has credited a possible meeting with an alien. Remembering her story, I was keen to relate the coincidence of seeing the lift sequence appear in an old sci-fi classic: 'The Day the Earth Stood Still.'

We were lying in bed quite awake having been talking of unrelated things. I remembered I wanted to mention the film and set about describing the story. When I had related to her the alien's halting of the lift and all power and further his message of the *futility of man's violent nature—we both at exactly the same moment were quietly 'startled' by drops of water falling directly into our open eyes. We were of course both surprised—me expecting something else to follow—it did not. We both exclaimed together we had experienced water falling in our eyes. No rain was falling. We lay motionless and silent for some time, watching and waiting. Both aware something special and irrational had occurred.*

We checked the ceiling immediately afterwards but could not see or feel any damp spots. The ceiling was painted white. It had not rained for a few days, and there had been a drought. Even when it rained heavily and over long periods, there were no leaks in this house.

1990: August (same bedroom)

I woke up feeling a strong presence of pure love. Paul suddenly exclaimed: 'I just felt a few drops on my arm!' I then told him about my beautiful feeling that lasted a few minutes. Over the next few days, I heard an inner voice telling me: 'It is your turn now.' I felt this message ('your turn') referred to both Paul and me.

While we lived at Hahndorf, I contacted an organisation in Adelaide that researched UFO phenomena. I was interviewed and described the encounter in the lift and some of my other mysterious experiences and was told these were of a spiritual nature.

Kanmantoo

1990: September

While Patrick was attending a college in Norway, Paul and I moved to the cottage we had built. It was an opportunity for us to experience a simple lifestyle with no power or mains water. I had two dreams during the time we lived there. In the first, I was showing a friend our one-roomed cottage made of rocks and mud brick. Upon entering, the room opened up into a Cathedral. The sight and feeling was glorious. I also had a lucid dream where I leapt across the hills with long strides, barely touching the ground.

1990: October

Around this time I noticed that my meditation (awareness) was continuous; no 'in and out' of focussed attention. One day I developed an unusually intense and persistent tickling sensation in the nostrils that disappeared after a few days.

1990: 24 October

In the evening, I had an inner knowing that from now on the focus of my meditation was to change—to be aware of God—the sacred stillness rather than my inner and outer world (objects of meditation). I also went to bed that evening with a feeling of satisfaction from having handed in my last assignment for a professional counselling course. I mention this because what happened next was so unexpected and so life-changing that it seems important to include what state of mind I was in at the time.

I woke up in the middle of the night overcome by vertigo. A tremendous force or energy had filled my whole body—a spinning sensation in the centre of the head made it impossible to move, and I was nauseated by the vertigo. I sat on the bed, feet on the floor while Paul held my hands, saying that he could feel the energy flowing through them. We sat like this for three hours before I was able to lie down. During this time we both heard a throbbing sound, and I could see a white light the size of a person from the corner of my left eye. It was these two phenomena that convinced us not to call an ambulance. I remember uttering, 'My God, my God!' In the face of this unknown and powerful force, which made my body feel like a completely hollow space, I placed my trust in the Higher Power. I spent three days in bed before I felt steady enough to walk around. My life quickly returned to normal with no apparent physical side effects from the ordeal that night. Again, I checked with my doctor who could only suggest a massive inner ear infection, despite there being no visible symptoms!

I had by then read about the Kundalini process but was left wondering whether, even if it was Kundalini, something had gone wrong, especially as I soon discovered that I had lost my emotional responses. For various other reasons, we had to sell our property soon after this event—a property that had been a labour of love—and here I was feeling no attachment at all. It was as if there was nothing left of me; photos from the past might as well have happened to someone else. I was unable to feel either disappointed or excited; in fact, wherever I went it was all the same. Going on a holiday to be inspired by beautiful scenery became meaningless. At first my family felt they had 'lost' me. Later they realised that they could see in my actions that I still loved and cared for them.

Woodside

1990: December

We were fortunate to make a quick sale and were able to move into our modern timber home in time for Patrick's return from Norway. We stayed in the Adelaide Hills so Patrick could complete his Year 12 at the same Steiner school he had attended before.

1991–92

Not long after we moved in, we had to change the phone for an older model because the handset of the new phone amplified the 'charge' in my brain. The increased sensitivity to certain sounds also necessitated the fridge being moved into the laundry. Initially I continued further study and also worked as a counsellor, but I soon discovered that anything involving concentration created a sensation of 'overheating' and intense 'tingling' in the brain. I found extensive conversation difficult. The effort of concentration overloaded the brain, and mentally I would blank out, unable to process the information. Words were listened to attentively, but nothing was retained. This 'charge' in the head also affected my short-term memory, and eventually I was forced to adopt a simple lifestyle based around the home.

The sudden shift into the present moment resulted in a deep-seated feeling of annihilation and compression in the solar plexus. Any inward-looking focus or attempt to move out of this state was impossible. I kept looking for an explanation as to what had happened. Thinking it might be a medical issue, I carefully ploughed through two thick volumes on psychiatry a friend had left behind after completing her studies. I found no illnesses that described the state I was in.

In my research I found these quotes: *What you describe as a completely emptied mind-substance devoid of energy or light, completely inert, is the condition of neutral peace and empty stillness which is or can be a stage of the liberation ... It is only by faith, aspiration and surrender that this self-opening can come.* (*Letters on Yoga, Vol. II* by Sri Aurobindo)

Emptiness is not a negative idea, nor does it mean mere privation, but as it is not in the realm of names and forms it is called emptiness or nothingness, or the Void. (*The Zen Doctrine of No Mind* by D.T. Suzuki)

That same year (1992), I was given the book *Dark Night of the Soul* by St. John of the Cross. It was a godsend! He writes that 'the Holy Spirit elevates the Soul from time to time relieving it of the agony of annihilation.' Messages like these offered hope and challenged the strong conditioning of the mind to label suffering in body or mind as pathological. I had not found any references to a sudden inflow of energy concurrent with a permanent shift into the present moment in any of my readings. After finding a description of annihilation to which I could relate, I no longer considered myself a total freak. Could the state I was in even be for the good?

1993

Gradually I became able to read more than a few paragraphs at a time. I had discovered a way of relaxing mentally the moment concentration reached my exhaustion point. I had stopped trying to explain my state to others, partly because the experience was hard to describe, but also because I had not realised that what I was going through was meaningful and worth sharing. I wanted to continue counselling (which included meditation instruction) but thought people would be put off if they knew what had happened to me.

1993: 28 July

I woke up during the night hearing an inner voice clearly saying, 'You are eligible for a demonstration'—another mysterious message, which I knew was not my own thought. Nothing happened, and I went back to sleep. In the early morning, I woke up feeling an inner glow of Pure Love. I lay still savouring this feeling. For a brief moment I felt alive again! It felt as if the fire of Love had thawed this frozen, lifeless state. This extraordinary event gave me hope that there was light at the end of the tunnel and that 'someone' was in charge of this process and knew what I could endure.

Around this time I was recommended to see a Jungian psychologist. His starting point was suggesting Alzheimer's disease. I was again reminded of the ignorance of professionals regarding altered states. During my year of consultations with him, I was at least able to talk to someone who was prepared to listen, and as I discovered books by Stanislav and Christina Grof (*Spiritual Emergency* and others), I could then pass this information on to my psychologist.

1993: September

Dream used in a Gestalt session with my psychologist: I dreamt that oil was poured on a piece of 'bread' so that it would levitate. The piece of bread was oval-shaped, about one inch thick, a bit smaller than my hand, light beige in colour and appeared crunchy. I did not see who poured the oil. I knew the bread levitated, without observing it. The psychologist asked me to identify with the bread in the dream.

> I said: 'The bread soaked up the oil, which made me lose my old form.'
> Then he asked: 'What would rise?'
> I found it hard to imagine that oil-soaked crumbs could levitate.
> I paused and said: 'The scent of baked bread could rise.'
> He asked: 'How did that feel?'
> I answered: 'It felt good. I am the presence of the ascent—no going back to old form.'
> The psychologist referred to anointing with oil as found in Leviticus, Chapter 8 in the Old Testament.

1994: May

I decided to seek advice from a Burmese meditation master, Sayadaw U Pandita, who was giving a thirty-day retreat in the Vipassana method. I discovered during the retreat that there was no opportunity for me to discuss anything as it was a silent retreat. We reported on our meditation practice daily, and Sayadaw U Pandita smiled approvingly when I reported on my neutral state. I was not used to meditating sitting crossed-legged, so spending eight hours a day sitting motionless became an exercise in transcending one's pain threshold—mindfully! Energy gradually built up during the retreat, creating a sensation of a 'solid' column or rod of energy extending down the spine. This phenomenon enabled me to sit fully supported during meditation; when pushing my back against this force I could 'click' into different positions, much like being in a reclining chair! I was told this energy was called *kriya*. I had noticed a person periodically jerking and bouncing while sitting in meditation and wondered if he was affected by the same force.

The intense practice of mindfulness brought repressed emotions to the surface. Meditators were often teary during sitting meditation. For me it was laughter that was repressed. One day I was listening to the swallowing of a person in the silent meditation hall. This was a new sound, and somehow I found that very amusing. I tried to be mindful while I left the hall and then burst out laughing outside. From then on, all sorts of situations triggered laughter. The teacher was not interested in what I found comical but asked me to describe the sensations in my body whenever I felt like laughing.

The strong 'charge' of heat, light and tingling vibration in the head seemed to create a 'veil' between me and the outside world. Was this the reason for the memory loss and lack of emotions? This question was not answered during the meditation retreat. (Due to interstate train and transport connections, I had to leave the day before the retreat ended, at which point speaking was allowed.)

Over time my memory gradually improved, not from concentration as before but by allowing memories and information to appear out of nothingness. The stillness was so profound (and still is) that it seemed like words and sentences just 'arranged' themselves there and then. I could read and have longer conversations without activating the 'charge' in the head. I still had lots of physical energy and lived an outwardly active and family-oriented life. In the company of others I was naturally cheerful, which meant this inner emptiness and 'al-one-ness' was totally invisible to others.

In 1994 I did an Activity Officers course. During this training, I volunteered at a large centre for patients with various brain injuries. Assisting with craft activities was meaningful, something I could do that did not require much mental concentration. The patients I worked with all had a label for their condition, and I thought they were very fortunate in the way they received assistance and support. In contrast, my 'disability' was invisible to others, and this deepened the feeling of annihilation and isolation.

These lines from D.H. Lawrence's poem 'Phoenix' reflect this devastating but transformational process:

Are you willing to be sponged out, erased, cancelled,
made nothing?
Are you willing to be made nothing?
Dipped into oblivion?
If not, you will never really change.

1995–96

I went to Norway early in 1995 to care for my mother, who had had a fall and was in hospital with a hip fracture. Not long after she had recovered from that, she had a second fall and was back in hospital. It was then decided she needed to be in a nursing home because my elderly father was not able to look after her at home. In order to assist with this transition, I stayed longer than planned.

During this time, I was finally reunited with Mikkel, my older son, who was now twenty-five. We had a lot of catching up to do! When it was time to return to Australia, Mikkel came with me. The extended stay in Norway had been a blessing. While I was in Norway, Patrick lived on campus at a university in northern New South Wales. It was here he had met his partner, Juliet, who was also doing a degree in music. When I heard they were expecting a baby, I decided to move to Lismore.

Lismore

In May 1996 I was back in Australia and moved in with Patrick and Juliet (to whom I had felt close from the day we met). I bought a duplex and had unpacked in time for the birth. Jasper was born in July, and I was pleased to be able to offer childcare in my own home. Coming back to look after a grandchild was life-giving. We both enjoyed the spontaneity of play, storytelling and song.

Paul, who had spent a few months with me in Norway, was back in Adelaide but later relocated to Lismore. We had a special reunion at Christmas, which also included Patrick's other half-brother (on his father's side) who travelled from Belgium to join us.

Mikkel, who had initially lived with me, moved in with his partner, and they had a son in September 1998. With their move interstate, I was not able to offer my other grandson, Ziggy, the same childcare I had offered Jasper.

1997

The unease resurfaced at times. It became a pointer, prompting me to look deeper. I did this in a state of surrender and trust in Divine guidance. I had learnt from Krishnamurti's teachings that the answer to a problem is in the problem. And so the unease, associated with emptiness and lack of identity, became my object of meditation. As I focussed on the unease, it grew in strength until one day a minor event triggered off a spontaneous 'rebirthing' experience. I curled up in a foetal position on the floor and cried, my breathing was rapid and rhythmical, and I watched while letting it all out. After a few minutes I felt peaceful. As I stood up, Paul (who had stood by concerned but not intervening) and I heard a chorus of birds singing as we had never heard before. At the time we didn't think to look outside to see if the birds were real, as we were both focussed on how quickly I had recovered. The next day, Paul and I climbed Mount Warning. As I rested my forehead against some of the big trees along the path, there was a lessening of the 'charge' in the head, together with a visionary experience of being one with the tops of the trees.

I have noticed a subtle feeling of a sacred presence in the depths of the state of nothingness. An inner quiet and receptiveness is needed to notice it. I am aware of the mind trying to recapture or recreate the right conditions for the sacred to stay but have discovered that it was neither in any object nor related to my environment. Whenever I tried to 'grasp' the sacred, all that happened was an increase in the 'charge' in the forehead.

There were times when I wondered if the predicament I was in was related to the encounter in the lift back in 1973. I decided to see a hypnotherapist to try and access more information about the mysterious person in the lift. Maybe I did see his face? And did something else happen that I had no memory of? During my initial interview, I decided to make an appointment for my first hypnotherapy session. That's when we heard three knocks on the door. The therapist was quick to open the door, but no one was there. When I turned up for my first session, the therapist was not there. It turned out that the date he had written on my appointment card was different to the date he had written in his appointment book. After these 'signs,' I decided it was unwise to pursue the identity of the stranger in the lift, which has remained a mystery.

1997: September

I attended a National Women's Spirituality Conference in New South Wales. I was hopeful that amongst the speakers representing various spiritual traditions, someone would mention the 'Void' or the 'Dark Night of the Soul,' but this did not happen. None of the speakers talked about a difficult process of inner transformation. I tried to share some of my experiences with a nun, but she could not relate to them and had not heard of the teaching of St. John of the Cross.

Dream: I hear the painful cry of a distressed bird outside in the street. I follow the sound and see a blue bird with its tail feathers caught in a closed door. I call out as I run over to the bird to release it. In its eagerness to escape, the bird tries to pull away and loses more feathers. Was my rushing over to help the bird contributing to more damage? Maybe I should have walked up to the bird without exciting it. The bird is happy to see me and eager to fly. I gather up the bird and hold it in my hands. I feel love and protection for it.

Phone call with my dear mother in Norway: During an extra-long phone call, my mother started to describe how empty she felt. She told me how her emotional connection with God had been absent for many years. I could empathise with her. Based on my own experiences and my understanding of the teaching of St. John of the Cross, I was able to offer her hope and a spiritual context for her anguish. This extended conversation was made possible because the staff at her nursing home forgot to come back to her room to help her put the phone down. I continued to talk to her (from Australia) until the staff arrived after about one hour. It was a blessing that we were given this extra time.

1998

Paul found a little notice in the local paper about a Spiritual Emergence Network (SEN) information meeting to be held in Lismore. He knew I would be interested. Some years previously I had read *The Stormy Search for the Self* and *Spiritual Emergency* by Stanislav and Christina Grof, the co-founders of SEN. I had made inquiries back then to see if there was a SEN group in Australia but was told there wasn't one.

When I rang Gini Witt, the coordinator of SEN, she told me that SEN Australia had been operating in Sydney and now that she had moved to Lismore she was keen to establish SEN here, if there was enough interest. This is how our paths crossed! The core group was formed after the initial informational meeting. We had had different experiences but shared a common vision. We agreed that spiritual emergence is a natural process of transformation that can produce symptoms and non-ordinary states, which can be perceived as pathological. Our aims were to support people in spiritual crisis ('Spiritual Emergency') and to educate both health professionals and the general public about the phenomenon of 'Spiritual Emergence.'

Spiritual Emergence can be defined as the movement of an individual to a more expanded way of being that involves enhanced emotional and psychosomatic health, ... and a sense of deeper connection with other people, nature and the cosmos. (The Stormy Search for the Self by Stanislav and Christina Grof. The Grofs are therapists and researchers in the field of personal transformation.)

SEN Australia in Lismore started up discussion and support groups. We also issued a quarterly journal, *Emergence*, with book reviews and personal accounts. Sharing stories was a way of validating and normalising our experiences as well as contributing to a better understanding of what the spiritual journey entails. (I was on the committee of SEN Australia [www.spiritualemergence.org.au] for ten years and have continued to be the contact person for people possibly undergoing the spiritual process of the Dark Night of the Soul.)

1999

The profound feeling of 'emptiness' that my mother described during our phone conversation in 1997 indicated to me that she was in the Dark Night of the Soul. During my last visit to Norway, she made a comment that stayed with me. She said regarding my father, her husband, that she was no longer attached to him. I understood that to mean she had finally detached from the 'idealised image'—the potential of the relationship. My mother was a deeply spiritual person who 'died to the world' before she physically passed away on 26 October at the age of ninety.

Therapy session with Karen Daniel (transpersonal and emotional release counsellor): I lay down on a mattress on the floor, relaxing and breathing, deeply and slowly. Karen sat behind me stroking my head. Soft music played in the background. Vibrational energy increased in the body, tingling from the tip of the big toe to the fingertips and head. Spasms started in the chest and solar plexus area. (These spasms sometimes woke me up at night.) I watched this energy, in a relaxed and open state. I thought of Paul and our phone call the night before and could feel his love and support for this session—then I felt teary. Karen encouraged me to make a sound with the crying, which I did while the spasms continued. Crying lasted a couple of minutes, then I was ready to laugh. I was aware of energy moving further down my body. Karen placed her hands on my stomach, asking me to go deeper into this sensation once the crying had stopped. I started making a very deep vocal sound, which reminded me of the sound of a didgeridoo! The spasms dissipated, but the vibrational tingling energy was still strong. Karen stroked the neck area and head.

Spasms built up again, and this time I started laughing. I observed that the spasms in the chest were the same as when

I cried. I made various sounds, more like chanting, until a clear note was produced. I went with the energy and let out a long note until that faded away. The tingling energy increased, and a bubbling, pulsating energy was felt in the fingertips and hands. Karen asked me to let my hands move freely if they wanted to. I waved them around, laughing and moving my head from side to side in a carefree fashion. Thumb and middle finger touched in a 'locked' position. Energy increased and the arms spontaneously moved up behind my head where Karen rested her hands on mine. The energy that had supported and suspended the arms above my head gradually dissipated, which allowed the arms to descend onto my chest. Energy then moved up to the centre of the head and this time a higher note came out. Then the energy increased in the vocal cords producing some strange yodelling. After a while, the yodelling changed into a clear, high note. Then Karen asked me to push my hands against hers to facilitate the release of the energy of this note. Spasm and energy moved to the belly while the sound I made was pressing against the eardrums.

When the session was over, I was feeling weak and dizzy and needed Karen to assist me while I walked out of the room. After resting for half an hour, I was lightheaded but in a peaceful state. Karen told me she had felt a lot of energy coming through my hands.

During this session, I had seen, with closed eyes, an image of an open eye inside a triangle. Later on I learned that this was the Eye of Horus: a symbol that represents the God enclosed, during the 'dead' period, awaiting rebirth. At the end of the session, Karen told me that the Kundalini energy was active and that the process could be trusted to take its natural course.

For years I had been buying Andrew Cohen's journal *What is Enlightenment?* In the very last issue I bought, Cohen wrote that 'enlightenment can go as deep as to affect the cellular level.' This comment made me wonder if that was the reason why, after reading his magazines for years, I had never come across any description of a process like mine. The articles I had read on enlightenment did not mention the physical effects or the intense suffering of annihilation from a permanent shift into the present moment. Was this because not-so-deep enlightenments don't produce these profound changes? Do most enlightenments happen more on a mental level? I wrote a letter to Andrew Cohen describing the state I was in and detailing some of the process. I was hoping for a reply to help explain what had happened to me. There was no reply.

I still don't know the answers to these questions.

1999: November

Support group with Karen Daniel using Sandplay therapy. Dialogue between two objects (symbols): I found it difficult to choose an object representing consciousness. In the end I decided on a picture of a 'goddess' with seven chakras and called that 'The Shiny One.' The other object was a naked clay figure posing as 'The Thinker.' Each person in the group had to choose two objects and take turns in sharing the dialogue between these two objects. According to my notes, my dialogue went something like this:

> *The Thinker: I can see you clearly, Shiny One. I ask you: What is the meaning of existence? My body is made of clay—and is perishable. But you, Shiny One,*

are made of light and belong to the cosmos. As The Thinker, I can recall the past and the future. I cannot be in the present. I am busy trying to find solutions to the many questions that arise. Tell me about your state, Shiny One. You look like you know from your own experience.

The Shiny One: I am consciousness, ever-present vastness, the nameless with no reference point within. I honour the sacred. If you stop the activity of thought, you can see that emptiness and consciousness are the same. Stand up tall—know what is true: let go of the image created by others or the image created by The Thinker. I am that which arises from moment to moment—stay with that. The sacred mystery will be revealed. All is Love.

A friend who knew of my state lent me Bernadette Roberts' book *The Path to No-Self*. This was the first time I had come across someone who had had a similar experience to me: the 'merging of the observer and the observed' and the inability to look inward. The unusual combination of a permanent shift into the Now concurrent with the powerful force of the Kundalini energy was still a conundrum.

In Jack Kornfield's book *A Path with Heart*, I found at least a mention of 'the dark night':

At the level of Insight meditation beyond pseudo-nirvana, the death-rebirth process becomes all-encompassing, involving our total being. After we abandon our spiritual identity, the meditation leads us through a total dissolution of a sense of self, through a 'dark night,' like death itself. To enter this path consciously challenges all we know of our identity. Yet it is the path to freedom.

In Sayadaw U Pandita's book *In This Very Life*, there was an explanation as to how mindfulness can lead to an unemotional state:

...Insight into the dissolution of phenomena.... Mindfulness is so agile now that it picks up the objects before the mind can begin to be perturbed by pleasantness or unpleasantness. There is no chance for attachment or aversion to arise.... The happiness of Nibbana occurs upon the cessation of mind and matter. It is the peace of the extinction of suffering. It is independent of contact with the six kinds of sense objects. In fact, it arises because there is no contact at all with sense objects.

I was fortunate to meet Lena McGregor, a local clairvoyant healer. I went to her initially because of the vibrational energy and pressure inside the top of the head as well as some anxiety and unease in the solar plexus. She identified the loss of personal self as liberation and congratulated me on my achievement! It was now possible, at last, to drop the mind's preoccupation with there being something wrong with me. Towards the end of the year, a new phenomenon appeared—a kind of high-pitched, bell-like ringing, a pleasant sound inside my head, which I mainly noticed at night.

1999: 10 December

I had a dream where I died. A man announced that my pulse had stopped. I was aware that, as I was about to die, my breathing would stop. As I realised that this was the end, I drew my last breath. To let my mother know that this was my very last breath, I placed my hand in hers. While expecting a gasp to follow, I woke up.

During the week that followed, the unease started to resurface. This was again a spiritual conundrum to be solved experientially, not mentally. For hours every day, I paced up and down the corridor in my home, needing to move physically while this deep 'enquiry' was going on. These attempts to look into the Void (emptiness) and observe the unease were exhausting. It all came to an impasse that ended in total surrender (to God). This was the last stage in a long process that culminated in what happened next.

1999: 17 December

During the night, I woke up suddenly when a force penetrated through the base chakra, climaxing with a blast of energy that shot up through the head. The next day I noticed that the physical feeling of confinement had ceased, as had the concentration of energy inside the top of my head. I also became aware that something had aligned itself behind the centre of the eyebrows. This manifested as seeing with 'one eye.' What had disappeared was the vibrational energy behind the forehead that I had felt for many years. This energy had created a sensation of being cross-eyed without in any way distorting my actual physical vision.

The mind was now at rest in the Ground of Being. This brought with it a profound sense of inner peace.... Beyond the personal self and the no-self is Pure Awareness—the sacred essence of consciousness.

2000

A constant 'tingling' sensation was now felt throughout the whole body. (In the past this internal sensation would move to different parts of the body, creating 'hotspots' of increased tingling and heat.) Whilst the mind was in a peaceful state, mental concentration created a sensation of 'overheating' the brain.

For a while I would wake up at night to find that I had stopped breathing. It was as if I had forgotten how to breathe. Fortunately, I always remained calm. I decided to see a doctor because breathing is important! He diagnosed sleep apnoea and referred me to a hospital with a sleep laboratory. As there were no other symptoms that fitted sleep apnoea (such as sleep deprivation), I was wondering if travelling interstate to undergo tests in a sleep laboratory was worth the trouble. That same day I had a 'chance' meeting in town with Lena McGregor, the clairvoyant healer whom I had seen in the past. I told her about the visit to the doctor and my uncertainty about further treatment. This led to a consultation where she offered an alternative explanation for my breathing problem. She could see that although the etheric channel was open and the Kundalini process was finished, the flow of energy in the throat chakra was restricted. She advised me to change my posture during the day as well as at night (tuck chin in, neck straight) and to look at any issue that needed voicing.

Lena also encouraged me to tell my story and to offer my experience to others. I sat with this thought of going public to see what I was supposed to do with it. I had noticed that whenever I shared what I knew to be true, my whole being felt vibrant and energised. I had also seen that my meditation practice had increased my awareness, helped to heal emotional wounds and erased old conditioning. Seeing that others could benefit from exploring a path of self-discovery, I decided to offer sessions in what I called 'Active Meditation' at the Healing Centre Lena was about to open. I also offered a 'Spiritual Emergence Forum' where people could meet and ask questions and where I would share my experiences.

2000: 26 May

Opening of Dhamata Healing Centre Lismore. Each practitioner gave an introductory talk at the Opening Day. Mine went like this:

> *The Active Meditation group is an opportunity for people to explore a more conscious way of living and to share insights along the way. My meditation practice started eighteen years ago after reading a book by Krishnamurti called Freedom from the Known. This book inspired me to start practising meditation: as in awareness of thoughts, feelings and actions—from moment to moment. I quickly became aware of the fact that I wasn't aware most of the time. That was a real insight!*
>
> *My first object of meditation was to do the dishes— with full awareness. This being a boring task, something*

to be done quickly to get on with more important activities, I became aware of the daydreaming, the thinking, planning ahead, while washing-up was done automatically. By bringing the awareness back on doing the dishes, I started to notice the beauty of the coloured, shiny soap bubbles—a foamy landscape continuously changing. The warm water caressing my hands.

We think it is efficient to do two or more things at the same time but, in fact, we are wasting both energy and an opportunity to experience what is really going on. There is a world of pure beauty revealed when the mind is silent. Paying attention to whatever is happening from moment to moment gives meaning to our lives.

The search for meaning is essentially a spiritual need. It is necessary to understand the mechanism of the mind or consciousness before we can talk about spirituality. In becoming aware of the content of consciousness, with all the conditioning which has shaped our likes and dislikes, we can see that so many of our actions and opinions are determined by this conditioning which comes from our particular upbringing, education etc. The benefit of practising meditation enables us to go beyond these reactive patterns and to identify with that which is 'behind' our emotional and mental activities. When we pay attention to what goes on in our mind, we will see that our mind is a bit like a radio or TV (if you are a visual person) playing recorded messages or lecturing about future events. This mind chatter prevents us from meeting each moment fully present. The activity of paying attention to what is going on, physically, emotionally and mentally, I call Active Meditation.

When you are totally absorbed in listening to music or watching a beautiful sunset, for instance, in those moments the mind is still—there are no thoughts, no past intruding. And when you shift your attention away from mental chatter and learn to observe the space between two thoughts, there is stillness. It is in this stillness that the Sacred dwell.

If you continue on this path of self-discovery, you will find that emotional feelings like pleasure and pain come and go like the movement of the pendulum. You cannot have one without the other. If in our everyday life we can be aware and present to all our feelings, we will find that eventually they lose their grip on us—the pendulum stops swinging. Eventually the Seeker may find what he or she was looking for—the Essence behind the phenomenal world, the Sacred Ground of Being.

After I had given individual sessions in Active Meditation for a while, two groups formed and met at my home. We focussed on spirituality and daily life with the emphasis on awareness and personal experience. The deep sharing that evolved was rewarding for us all.

2001: 11 September

I was sitting at the dining table by the window paging through my book of notes and quotes. Just as I was reading the words

'The Creator is not separate from creation,' a rainbow lorikeet flew straight into the tall window in front of me and dropped to the deck. It took a few minutes before the dazed bird could fly off. (From where I was sitting, I had often watched the lorikeets having a splash in a bowl of water on the deck. During the five years I had lived there, I had only once seen a bird hit the window.) The radio was on, and I heard the shocking news that a plane had hit the World Trade Center in New York. The reporter expressed great sadness for the people who were in the building at the time. It made me think of the people on the plane who saw what was about to happen and their horror at not being able to prevent it. I imagined they would have died on impact, maybe in a state of shock and confusion at being in a new realm— not everyone has considered the possibility that consciousness can survive death. I prayed for the souls of all these people and then walked down stairs. A little while later, as I was walking back up the stairs, a lorikeet crashed into the other tall window (this window was to the left of the window hit by the first bird).

Later, when I turned the TV on, I found out that there had been another plane crash into the second tower of the World Trade Center. The images were surreal: two planes flying purposefully into the Twin Towers! I was then reminded of the extraordinary timing of the two birds that had crashed into my windows. These two narrow windows formed columns of glass from floor to ceiling. What had happened was that one bird flew into the middle of the right window followed by the second bird crashing into the left window, only minutes apart. This was eerie. I thought of the quote I had been reading just before the announcement of the first plane hitting the first tower: 'The Creator is not separate from creation.' God is with us on our journey—thank God for that!

Dream: The choir I belong to is ready to perform on stage. Some are dressed in yellow; I look down and realise that I am dressed in blue. Yellow and blue must be the dress code for this performance. The show is delayed, and we are asked to wait outside. In the sky I can see a flock of brown birds in the distance. They are flying in formation and look like wedge-tailed eagles. When they come closer I can see they are people with wings flying in unison—two at first, then one of these human birds flies just above my head. Their faces are beaming with joy. The sight is a pure delight to watch. (I sing with an a cappella choir called 'The Joy of Singing.')

Coming home one night after performing with the choir, I was shocked to discover I had been burgled. The feeling of elevation and joy suddenly dropped, and I felt ice cold when I opened the front door and saw the muddy footprints on the carpet and objects missing. I was living on my own at the time. This home invasion was instrumental in me wanting to move away from the area.

Serendipity

2001–03

Paul and I had a history of both living together and living apart. We had a passionate and loving relationship that was marred by Paul's unpredictable outbursts of anger.

Paul had a calm and caring side to his personality that could suddenly change. He would discharge his anger, either blaming me or outer circumstances. Over time, I found I was unable to tolerate walking on eggshells and we separated, but we were soon drawn back together again. Paul had been participating in my Active Meditation group where he had spoken openly about his anger issues. I took that to mean he was now owning his anger and was hopeful he would observe his anger rather than verbally projecting it.

While visiting friends living in Serendipity, a multiple occupancy (land-sharing) community in northern New South Wales, they told us that there was a share for sale. I decided to move to Serendipity with Paul, hoping that now we would be more proactive in changing patterns of behaviour. Again, we had chosen a very physical lifestyle that was, in some ways, a repetition of Kanmantoo thirteen years ago. This time we didn't start from scratch—a little mud-brick cottage was already there, and instead of tree planting, we had to have trees cut down to clear an area around the cottage. We put a lot of energy into transforming our dilapidated cottage into a charming home. Paul found it especially satisfying white-washing the interior mud-brick walls and clearing the block of felled trees. However, whenever things didn't go according to plan, there would be another drama—the option of Paul observing his anger wasn't happening. I had noticed that there were periods of time when Paul looked sad and vacant and angered more easily. Over time, I came to understand that we were dealing with a deep-seated issue.

Paul grew up in a family with an English father, an Italian mother and grandmother and a younger brother. Paul's parents were happy together, and he said he felt loved but also controlled by the two females at home. He has few memories from his early childhood. He had congenital cataracts, which meant that as a child he was limited in what activities he could do or was allowed to do. From an early age, Paul got used to projecting his anger and frustration onto others.

In my family, we rarely expressed or even discussed emotions. My father looked depressed but was not an angry man. I had mixed feelings about my father—I looked up to him and knew he loved me, but I also felt uneasy around him. My mother once said she was too kind; I think she was implying she was too submissive. I never saw my parents have an argument. It was not what was said but what was unsaid that created a rather oppressive atmosphere in the home. I often wished my parents had separated.

During our first year at Serendipity, we experienced extreme weather conditions—from a drought to a cyclonic storm to a huge bushfire. The fire, which started in the national park surrounding the community, spread and became an inferno due to strong and changeable winds. There were fewer firefighters than usual due to it being Boxing Day and only one access road, which we knew wasn't an option. Together with other residents, we managed to survive in a clearing in the forest while the fire raged all around us. Homes were saved, but a vast area was left completely black due to the intensity of the fire.

The transformation in nature of this now blackened and smoke-filled environment was unlike anything we had previously experienced. The first grass to emerge in the black ash was iridescent green. Wild flowers appeared after soaking rain, and new shoots on the trunks of scorched gumtrees promised new life. I was overly keen to clear the ground of debris after the fire to make room for regrowth. I knew that I was discharging the energy of frustration around the unresolved issues in our relationship, but I still overdid it and strained my back.

The fire was a catalyst for change. Up until the fire, I had been charging ahead, building and renovating. After the fire, the need to 'renovate' (both home and relationship) had ceased. It had run its course, and I knew it was time to leave. I decided to move to a lifestyle village for those over fifty on the mid-north New South Wales coast and ordered a manufactured home. As it turned out, I had to wait nine months before the house was ready. While waiting for the house to be completed, I was still hoping things would shift. Nothing changed, however, as Paul still reacted to situations from his unconscious self while I tried to dialogue with his rational self. Having a partner with so much emotional volatility taught me to be centred in the stillness within.

Staying on at Serendipity for nine months was traumatic but conducive to spiritual growth. I could see that I had unrealistic expectations—caught up in an 'idealised image' of what the situation would look like if it changed for the better. In my weakened state and with my dreams shattered, there was now less resistance. For me, this was a time of surrendering.

Valla Beach

2003

In July I was told my house was ready, and I left Serendipity, travelling with the removalist to Valla Beach. On arrival, I found the steps up to the front door were missing! The manager had told me the house had been completed and cleaned, but instead it was a dusty mess inside and still needed tradespeople to finish off the on-site work. As usual, I was observing my reactions. The feeling of being let down did not linger—I could get on with the job at hand without the emotional fallout.

Once the house was completed, I was able to relax in my new abode. I had stopped driving years ago and had chosen this particular village because the beach was an easy stroll away and I could do my shopping using the weekly village bus. I was fortunate to meet people in the village who offered to take me to choir rehearsals and to yoga classes. In time, my back improved and I could take on a plot in the community vegetable garden. I continued as secretary and support person for SEN.

At times I experienced a laryngeal spasm, which made it impossible to breath in or out. If I happened to swallow into the trachea, the epiglottis muscle would close and cut off the airway. When the spasms struck and breathing stopped, it was impossible to make a sound. All I could do was totally relax and wait for the airway to open, which always seemed a very long time. I consulted a doctor who did a swallow test and examination, which showed no abnormalities. The doctor was confident that it wouldn't kill me: if I fainted the throat would eventually open, he said reassuringly! So in terms of spiritual practice, this condition brought me to my knees (less distance to fall should I faint) while surrendering to God's will and mercy.

Paul stayed on at Serendipity until our share sold and then went back to Lismore where he continued his counselling studies. Later on, he became the coordinator of an organisation that deals with relationship issues and runs programs for men with anger issues wanting to change their behaviour. Paul and I had constructive dialogues over the phone and stayed in touch by visiting each other. The deep love and sense of commitment we shared made it possible to live separately without growing apart. The mystical experiences we had shared in the past (such as the drops in our eyes with the announcement that 'now it is your turn') made me see our relationship in a spiritual context. I realised our lives were intertwined and we were on a mission—together.

2003: 27 November

I sat down at home to write a personal loan agreement between myself and a good friend. She was in financial difficulties, and I was glad to be able to help her out (she needed the money more than I did). Although I had no need to think she would not honour her commitment to repay me, it had occurred to me that in the event that one of us died before the loan was repaid, our relatives needed to know about this loan. I was to write and sign this agreement and post it for her to sign. Slowly I started writing 'I…,' intending to write 'Marie Gundersen.' Instead of Marie, I wrote Mary! I had never misspelled my name, and no one had ever called me Mary. I tore up the paper and started again, slowly and with great focus. Again, after 'I,' the name Mary appeared on the paper. Obviously I wrote it, but how I could make this mistake twice was perplexing! The third time, I completed the contract with my real name.

Later on, I started to wonder if this unusual misspelling of my name was another mystical experience with a message for me. I did not know what to make of it. After recording it in my journal, I forgot all about it. A year later, a visitor lent me a book on the lives of St. John of the Cross and St. Teresa of Ávila. There I came across, for the first time, the expression 'Martha and Mary' (from the Bible), used to signify the doer and the listener—Mary being the contemplative. It then dawned on me that being made to write the name Mary could be linked to that. There were times when I had wondered if my loss of motivation and desire to engage in worldly pursuits was unhealthy. Discovering the meaning of the name Mary in this book and the contemplative dimension of the scriptures certainly offered an explanation for my state. Maybe writing my name as Mary on an 'official' document was done to show me that this state of being was a new stage and should be seen in a spiritual context rather than being pathologised.

The shift in 1990 into the present moment has affected me in all aspects of daily life. In this state I am no longer motivated by emotions or driven to achieve personal goals. I have no desire to go on holiday or to seek entertainment, and I do not desire food, yet I still have an appetite and eat a balanced diet. The nervous system is sensitised and concentration can 'overheat' the brain. In a worldly sense, I have become quite ineffective—unable to drive, study or use the Internet. At the same time there is an increased vibrancy and vitality, with less need for sleep.

During a singing lesson, my teacher once asked me to express the emotion in a romantic song, but that was not possible for me—emotions were not something I could relive. I had no words to describe this state and how 'empty' I was, so I resumed singing in the hope that the sentiment was in there somewhere. I was learning to read music and found I was able to focus on that, whereas other forms of concentration led to overload. With my teacher's encouragement, I joined a classical choir that performed major classical works, including Bach's Mass in B Minor.

I also joined a local bush-walking group. I used to walk in the middle of the line of people, as I felt overwhelmed by the prospect of being left behind. I was in a 'fragile' state, feeling as vulnerable as a newborn child, totally dependent on others for protection. This was not a psychological issue but due to my formless state. The absence of emotional responses also affected my bush-walking experience. Whenever someone enthusiastically pointed out a beautiful view, I hid the fact that I could not share in their excitement. I had stopped trying to explain my state to others as it was hard to describe and easily misinterpreted. Nevertheless, in the present moment, I enjoyed the companionship and the adventures we shared.

Sufi teacher Hidayat Inayat Khan said: *The higher the mystic reaches in his or her inner evolution, the more difficult it is to adjust to worldly conditions. ... Mysticism implies communicating with others on their own level...*

2004–06

When I found out that there was going to be a week-long retreat on St. Teresa of Ávila at a Carmelite monastery, I wanted to be part of it. I had read some of St. Teresa's writing and knew she and St. John of the Cross were contemplatives of the Carmelite Order. I was hopeful that there I would meet others who had personally experienced the 'Dark Night of the Soul.'

Before I went to the retreat, a Catholic friend had told me that, as a non-Catholic, I should not receive the Eucharist. At the first Mass I asked if I could sit and observe at the back of the church, but the priest, who was also the director, said he wanted me to be included. Participating in the Eucharist made me feel compromised and vulnerable. All the rituals were foreign to me, and I was concerned about acting irreverently out of ignorance. Afterwards I discovered that some people had felt uneasy about me, as a non-Catholic, receiving the Eucharist.

We were shown a film of St. Teresa's life—a beautiful production filmed in Spain. Each day, after we had watched a section of this film, the director commented on the film and made some interesting observations from his own travels in Spain. (Places looked familiar to me—at age sixteen, I had travelled throughout Spain on a holiday with my mother, aunt and uncle. I remembered my uncle, who was interested in history, asking if I would like to visit a monastery in Toledo where St. John of the Cross had been imprisoned in 1577. I declined. Years later I learned that it was here he wrote the poem 'The Dark Night of the Soul.')

The director's talks were very interesting and informative but lacked an understanding of her spiritual (mystical) state. I thought quotes by St. Teresa of Ávila, which I wrote down while watching the film, related to her own Dark Nights: *How long shall I wait to see your presence?* We saw her clawing at the picture of Christ, falling to her knees in desolation… *I am wounded, but you don't give me the remedy…. The soul rests in rest. It understands Nothing…* The director interpreted that to mean she was confused and had no one to talk to. Teresa was just lonely like we all are at times, he said, and her saintliness was due to her monastic life. When Teresa reached the spiritual marriage of the seventh mansion, it was explained as a friendship with God.

I had come to the retreat hoping to hear about the 'Dark Night of the Soul' and meet others to share this experience with, but neither the director nor any of the thirty participants mentioned it. I realised I had assumed the Dark Night was a common phenomenon and that here amongst Catholics I would meet people who had experienced this process. During the retreat, I would have liked to have offered my own explanation for Teresa's suffering. I felt she spoke of a profound emptiness far deeper than the experience of emotional loneliness. When the retreat was finished and the director was giving me a lift to the station, I decided to mention that I disagreed with his interpretation that Teresa was confused and lonely when she said that her soul 'understands Nothing.' I felt she meant emptiness as in the Dark Night of the Soul. However, he saw no link between her and St. John of the Cross and maintained that her suffering was the kind of suffering and loneliness we all go through.

Prior to the retreat, I had been told that there was a priest at the same Carmelite Centre to whom I could talk about the Dark Night of the Soul. I met with this priest during the retreat, and I attempted to describe the state I was in. He responded by telling me that this state was 'good' but that there would be more purging. He also advised me not to try and understand God. That made a lot of sense to me! I also mentioned to him that I had wanted to join the Carmelite Monastery in Lismore a few years earlier and that during an interview I had been told that their experience was that women my age were set in their ways. The priest seemed surprised to hear that I was considered too old.

The idea that I could go to a monastery and be part of a spiritual community sustained me through the years of suffering emptiness and annihilation (1990–99). My more recent thinking had been that in a monastic setting, I would now have something to offer by giving others hope and encouragement. I realised that I had been naive to assume that entry into a monastery was straightforward for a person in my state. Finding others to share the spiritual journey with, whether in a monastery or in the world, wasn't as easy as I had assumed.

Only if we venture repeatedly through zones of annihilation can our contact with Divine Being, which is beyond annihilation, become firm and stable. The more a man learns wholeheartedly to confront the world which threatens him with isolation, the more are the depths of the Ground of Being revealed and the possibilities of new life and Becoming opened.
—The Way of Transformation by Karlfried Graf Dürckheim

Over the years, Paul played an important role in providing me with books from different traditions. In 2004 I was given the book *Ask the Awakened* by Wei Wu Wei as a gift from Paul. I felt the author described my experience and the state I was in, although there was no mention of a force or energy. Wei Wu Wei said, 'Enlightenment is not the attainment of anything whatsoever. It is purely subjective. Pure subjective awareness is outside the seriality of time.'

For so long, the conundrum had been why I was unable to 'self-reflect.' This was the result of the shift into the Now (in 1990), the moment when 'I,' the subject and the object, merged and time 'ended.' (Krishnamurti said that 'Time is the interval between the observer and the observed.') This 'merger' happened on a cellular level and took years to integrate. Towards the end of this stage, I was aware of both emptiness and a sacred presence (fullness).

Wei Wu Wei said: 'The term "Void" gives an indication of an eye looking at itself and seeing nothing' and 'When the awakened desist from looking—they ARE...' The inability to look inward was exhausting. I realised I had tried to objectify my inner nature. It all came to an impasse (in 1999) where I surrendered to God—that which is not an object but the essence of consciousness. After I stopped trying to 'self-reflect,' which was like looking into the Void—impossible because I was not separate from what I was looking at—I experienced a force ascending through my body and I was released into a state of Pure Awareness.

Wei Wu Wei said: 'The absence of an absence is a presence [double negative].... Absence implies and requires the Presence of that which cannot be named, because named it would thereby become an object...' This relates to an analogy I had used when trying to explain to others what it is like to live in the Now—a state without the 'flavours' of emotional feedback: Imagine drinking pure water for the first time. Until then, all you know is the different tastes of flavoured water. Then when all the flavours are taken away, unflavoured water seems rather dull. For some time, the awareness is of the absence of flavours. Gradually the absence dissipates and the purity of the water is noticed. Pure Awareness is the essence of consciousness—it is pure because of the absence of the absence of the flavours!

In 2004, when I discovered 'The Complete Works of Saint John of the Cross,' it gave me the impetus to look for a spiritual connection in the contemplative tradition of Christianity here in Australia. I searched the Internet and with Paul's help found the Camaldolese, a contemplative branch of the Order of St. Benedict. This led me to Father Michael Mifsud, the Prior and Regional Chaplain for the Australian and New Zealand Camaldolese Oblates. (Oblates are not monks or nuns but have an association with monastic communities.)

Oblate spirituality seeks above all else a loving union with God through a full, prayerful life: a life which is at the same time both deeply interior and outwardly expansive in love and service of neighbour.... The encounter with God in silence and solitude is distinctive of our tradition. (Introduction to the Rule for Camaldolese Benedictine Oblates)

It was on Father Michael's advice that I looked into becoming a member of the Catholic Church. This was a new direction for me. From when I was very young, I knew that a Divine presence sustained me. It had not occurred to me that this inner presence was the same God spoken of by the Church. In conversation with Father Michael, I was able to validate my experiences within a Christian context. He felt I had a genuine mystical union with God. This acknowledgment was very helpful as I had seen myself as a freak for so long. Joining the Camaldolese Benedictines and attending Oblate retreats fulfilled a need to belong to a spiritual tradition. Their commitment to inter-religious dialogue also appealed to me.

In the book *Universal Wisdom* by Bede Griffiths, I found a description of the Trinity to which I could relate: *The Father;*

the Ground and Source of being, expresses himself eternally in the Son; the Word or Wisdom, which reveals the Godhead, and the Holy Spirit is the energy of love, the feminine aspect of God, by which the Godhead eternally communicates itself in Love.

I felt I could 'comprehend' the paradox of the triune God, the Three in One and One in Three, because in the state of 'Pure Subjectivity' I am conscious of the whole without the split of subject and object.

Before I converted, I had read an extract from Vatican II on Religious Liberty that said: 'Nobody must be forced to act against their conscience.' With little background in the workings of the Church as an institution, I found this reassuring.

After a time of discerning what I was meant to do, I commenced a RCIA (Rites of Catholic Initiations for Adults) program, which took about seven months. Sister Patricia, our parish nun, led regular RCIA meetings held in my home. At the end of this free program, there was no pressure to convert. I decided to join the Church, a decision that was also influenced by the vision of the cross back in 1976. Leading up to my conversion, I underwent three rites of healing and received blessings during Mass. After the conversion, at Easter 2006, I continued to attend weekly Mass.

I was introduced to the teachings of Father Thomas Keating at the 2006 Oblate retreat through watching some of his DVDs on Centring prayer. (Contemplative prayer is not about words but rather about being available, consenting to the Divine presence and action within.) Realising he was an outstanding teacher, I started reading his books on the contemplative dimension of Christianity (www.contemplativeoutreach.org). At Oblate retreats I had learnt to do the Divine Office, a Catholic daily prayer used in monasteries (also called the Liturgy of the

Hours). Reading the Divine Office in the morning and evening became an intrinsic part of my spiritual life.

I make regular trips to Queensland to visit family. This takes a lot of organising as there was a split in the family early on due to the very different values and lifestyles of my two sons. This split meant that the two cousins, Jasper and Ziggy, lost contact.

When my grandchildren were in primary school, I made each boy a little 'Book of Life' with drawings to illustrate the meaning of life. I wanted to imbue in both of them a sense that there is a spiritual dimension to life. Here is a sample of what I wrote:

> *God is the force in nature that makes everything grow. Within a very tiny seed of a huge gumtree there is a tremendous force that prompts its growth. Seeds grow in darkness, establishing their roots before the plant shoots through the surface. Nurtured by sunlight and water, each seed—encoded with its unique characteristics—keeps growing until the seed reaches its potential. Within all of us is our soul or 'glow of awareness.' This inner 'glow' is connected to God—the source of Love and Light, which sets in motion our journey of self-discovery programmed to seek wholeness and fulfilment.*

I also wanted to convey my understanding of spiritual matters to Mikkel, who saw himself as an atheist. Here are extracts from my correspondence to Mikkel:

My scientific mind thinks of it this way: phones and computers send images and messages through space. We know that telepathy, sending mental messages to others, also works. That is pretty amazing. Prayer is a form of telepathy. I am sceptical about anything that is not based on personal experience, so I have put this thing with prayer to the test many times. I found that both in despair and when asking for guidance, there has been a response—I have changed or the situation has changed. How prayer works is a mystery, just like electricity is a mystery—we can see the effect of it, but we don't know the origin of it. It just is—created but not by us. Christ, the physical manifestation of the divine source (God), came to assist anyone who sincerely asked for help. After the resurrection, Jesus said he would send the Holy Spirit to guide us and give us peace in the midst of our suffering. He came especially for the broken-hearted and lonely, the exiled and marginalised, because they are closer to surrendering to God, unlike the successful who are lost in their material comfort and self-inflation. Something for your reflection…

Mikkel succumbed to a lifestyle of substance abuse years ago. (He has asked me to include this in my book.) Sometimes I was faced with my own limitations of what I could do, and I learned to 'hand it over' prayerfully, not thinking about solutions but resting in sacred silence. In that state I prayed for Mikkel to be divinely guided and protected from harm. Mikkel loved his son and stopped using heroin so he could have custody of Ziggy. This was a heroic act. Since then I got to know my real son and we have developed a close and trusting relationship. Thanks to support from Ziggy's other grandmother, many of their struggles were alleviated. Despite dramas and chaos in Ziggy's life, he was able to complete his Higher School Certificate (Year 12) and did well.

Paul and I would visit each other regularly. We also talked daily on the phone, sometimes counselling each other if needed. It has been invaluable to be able to describe my inner state and the effects it has on my daily life. Paul can hear me, even if he cannot relate to this state. Not living together allowed space to pause and reflect whenever old patterns reappeared. Paul found and passed on to me a brilliant book, *The Verbally Abusive Relationship: How to Recognize it and How to Respond*, by Patricia Evans. The following quote illustrates the difference between a healthy relationship and an abusive one:

> *Verbal abuse is a violation, not a conflict. There is a difference between conflict and abuse. In a conflict each participant wants something different. In order to resolve the conflict, each discusses their wants, needs and reasons, seeking a creative solution. There may not be a solution, but no one forces, dominates or controls the other.*

As a child, I had my boundaries violated and learned to normalise conflicting feelings towards my father. This was a core issue that made it hard for me to set healthy boundaries. Reading this book helped me to recognise and name the unease I felt around inappropriate behaviour. Despite us living apart, this issue was not resolved—it seems that we both needed more opportunities and greater insights to change patterns of behaviour.

Occasionally I am contacted through SEN to assist people with experiences possibly related to the Dark Night of the Soul. People appreciate that I take time to listen and validate their stories, and it is good to know I have something to offer. I find it helpful to use examples of how nature heals. When someone is depressed or feels that life is meaningless, I tell them: 'We can all observe how an open sore is repaired by the growth of new skin. In time, our emotional wounds will heal too. Healing is innate in Nature.'

Increasingly I had become aware of the misuse of the term 'Dark Night of the Soul' when used to describe an experience of depression. This prompted me to write an article based on my own experiences and understanding of St. John of the Cross's teachings.

Contemporary writings and references to the Dark Night of the Soul often focus on the early stages (the Night of Sense). St. John of the Cross's poem 'The Dark Night of the Soul' describes the latter stage. He writes that many will start the Night of Sense but that few will be called to the deeper purifications of the Night of Spirit.

Gini Witt, had asked if I could write an update of my own spiritual journey. Thanks to her encouragement and skilful editing, the two articles, *A Modern Mystic* and *St. John of the Cross and the Dark Night of the Soul*, were published in *Emergence* in 2007. Due to me not being connected to the Internet and Gini living in Lismore, we used to do a lot of the editing over the phone, which took many months.

In the editorial of the issue of *Emergence* in which my articles appeared, Gini wrote: *Writing and editing the St. John of the Cross article took far longer than I had expected. The finished product involved Marie digesting the contents of a very long book, full of complex spiritual concepts, then imparting it to me and, even more difficult, the two of us working to get this information into a reader-friendly format.*

When I was writing the article on St. John of the Cross, I showed the draft to Sister Patricia. She commented that depression and the Dark Night can overlap, and I included this. After she moved to a retirement village, we continued to correspond. Her replies to my letters were always caring and thoughtful. She was familiar with the writings of Father Thomas Keating and believed him to be a holy man.

2007–08

Something extraordinary occurred when I started typing the article 'A Modern Mystic' for *Emergence*. Being inexperienced, I did not know about the key to lock in capital letters. Yet, part of a sentence appeared in capitals: 'The two of us… travelled FROM THE GROUND FLOOR TO THE SEVENTH FLOOR. When I left the lift, he mysteriously vanished.'

When I looked at what I had typed, I was surprised, as I would have needed to press 'Caps Lock' twice for this to happen, and I knew I had not done that. I realised this was another mystical experience with a message, which was to pay attention to the number of floors we travelled in the lift. I could see a link between the seven floors and the seven chakras and a link between the ascending lift and energy ascending from the base chakra to the crown chakra.

When Kundalini awakens, the coiled energy is believed to raise like a serpent from the base, transforming the natures of the six chakras in its path, and ultimately moving through the crown of the head into Sahasrara chakra. This makes possible the experience of God-realization or enlightenment.
—*Energies of Transformation. A Guide to the Kundalini Process* by Bonnie Greenwell, PhD

In 1990 I was 'hollowed out' by an unknown energy, and in 1999 I had another experience with a powerful energy that opened up a channel for the inflow of Divine Light. (This spiritual Light cannot be perceived by the senses and is different to clairvoyant sight.) A body that has been 'hollowed out' is like a house where all the furniture and belongings have been removed. It looks as if nobody lives there anymore. The purpose of moving out all this clutter is to clean the house. Once the windows are cleaned and the sun shines brightly into the empty space, it reveals dust and cobwebs not noticeable before. This metaphor illustrates how the inflow of Divine Light highlights all impurities. In this state where the mind is often silent, even a fleeting self-centred thought does not go unnoticed. I am convinced that it is the presence of God's Pure Love and Light that causes any contrasting impurities in me to be highlighted and amplified. I found this quote by St. Alonso, a Spanish mystic, which seems to describe the same Divine Light: *When the love of God enters the soul, it shows up all our faults as a sunbeam shows up every particle of dirt. The same light which reveals the splendour of God reveals our own vileness.*

2009

Since the shift in 1990, I have had a recurring dream: I am alone at night in a city; it is dark and desolate. Sometimes there are people in the distance, but I cannot reach them.

When on my own, the state of tranquillity is sometimes overshadowed by a loneliness that is related to feeling a disconnect with the world around me. Over the years, I had often yearned to live in a monastic setting where I imagined people like me were meant to be. Seeing the film of St. Teresa of Ávila's monastic life in 2004 deepened my yearning to be part of a spiritual community.

Someone I was associated with was talking about forming a new monastery, and I expressed my interest. After being accepted, I followed the progress of this interstate project. When the leader had found someone else interested in joining, I put the house up for sale and started preparing to move. After some months when the house hadn't sold, I decided to pack up and leave anyway, hoping a buyer would turn up soon.

Not long after my arrival, it became obvious the community was not ready to start. I was housed with only one other woman, and I found that the only other members of the community, the leader and the priest, were living miles away. The four of us only met briefly at morning prayer, and for the rest of the day the other woman and I were left on our own. It turned out she was prone to unprovoked outbursts of anger, and in my open state of awareness, I was unable to stay in such a hostile environment. When I found out that the truck with my furniture was still on the mainland, I asked the driver to return to Valla. Then I had to promptly make arrangements to be back before my furniture arrived, as the driver required a cash payment on delivery. I explained my reasons for leaving, and for leaving in such a hurry, to the person in charge and asked him to keep me informed about the development of the community. I felt at peace with my decision to leave. I did not feel a need to criticise despite the fact that this had been an exhausting and costly 'detour.'

The fallout was unexpected. I was publicly misrepresented and shamed for leaving, which was presented as having led to the closure of the community. I felt burdened by the blame and took on the shame for having caused the closure. Being present to these feelings assisted the healing of old wounds. I had learned that wounds need to be triggered so that the Light can penetrate the deepest reaches of the hurt. The Divine Light both highlights and purifies.

One day I discovered a strange creature in my garden that looked like a small pine cone covered in sticks. I had never seen anything like it. I watched the 'thing' move across the driveway and saw a little head sticking out from the cone. When I picked 'her' (?) up, her head disappeared and the opening closed. I decided to place her on the back deck so she would not get squashed. The next day I found the stick creature high up on a timber post at the deck. She had climbed to the top of the post and left behind a white trail that looked like a ladder! I checked on her every day, but the cocoon was closed and did not move from there. I learned from a visit to the local library that the 'stick creature' was a Bagworm moth caterpillar, which lives inside a case made of plant material. I named her 'Mottie.'

Sometime later I noticed another, smaller 'Mottie' attached to the rim of the roof gutter. I decided to move this caterpillar so it wouldn't become easy prey for a bird. Part of the body was sticking out from the cocoon and glued to the metal surface. I removed 'him' as gently as I could and placed him on the deck next to the post where the other 'Mottie' was attached. The next day he was nowhere to be seen. Coming back from the garden, I stepped onto the doormat and noticed what I thought was a piece of 'Mottie' in one of the holes of the black rubber mat. The piece looked smaller than what I had moved. I was saddened by this sight, thinking some critter had eaten part of him and that I could have caused his death by interfering. Maybe he would have survived if I had left him attached to the gutter. Although I had acted in good faith, I had failed in my attempt to save him, I thought. With tears in my eyes, I said sorry to this broken piece and buried him in the ground. Somehow that didn't feel right, so I dug him up and placed him in the flower pot by the back door. Later on, I had another look at this 'dead piece' and noticed a movement! In case a breeze had created this slight movement, I placed the piece in a more sheltered part of the flower pot. I also prayed that there was life in there and breathed on it! When I checked the next day, the piece had shifted position. This smaller 'Mottie' was alive!

It had been a privilege to watch how nature reflects spiritual transformation. My fascination with 'Mottie,' enclosed in her case, was symbolic of my own 'entombment.' The 'dismembered Mottie' in the 'black hole' reminded me of my own brokenness and isolation, and my teary reaction to the death I thought I had caused was also related to a tendency to take on blame.

2010

The subject of Kundalini had come up in conversation with an oblate, and I remembered I had read an ebook titled *Kundalini Energy and Christian Spirituality*. I looked through my folders and found a copy of the ebook cover together with a letter I had written in 2005 to the author, Philip St. Romain. I had wanted to give some feedback to the author, but my email would not 'send.' Five years later, when I looked at the cover of the ebook, I now noticed it included a quotation from Thomas Keating! Thomas Keating had written: 'This book will initiate Christians on the spiritual journey into this important but long neglected dimension of the transforming power of grace.'

I wrote a letter to Father Thomas Keating in September 2010. Here is an extract:

> *I am grateful for this quote, which together with the writing helped to place aspects of my own inner process in a Christian context. The world at large needs to rediscover and redefine the spiritual dimension; to inform science, education, politics and religion etc. I sense a certain urgency to respond to this need and wonder if in collaboration with others, my own story and experiences may be useful?*

In my letter, I also thanked him for his invaluable contributions to the contemplative life and included the SEN journal containing my two articles. Father Thomas Keating's reply was most unexpected!

October 26, 2010
Dear Marie,

I received and have read your articles and encourage you to consider sharing more of your experience for the very reasons you give in your letter. Anyone overtaken by the awakening of kundalini will be interested in hearing your Christian experience of it. Perhaps you will feel inspired to enlarge on these two articles or use them as a basis for a book with a lot more details. Those you have shared are very helpful and well written.
In Christ's love, Thomas Keating

I had no ambition to write a book, but I felt validated. His encouragement made me feel it would be worth saving some of this material, so I started to sort through my old notes and diaries. (This was the beginning of our correspondence. Some of these letters are copied in the Appendix.)

2011–12

Living in the world in my state was difficult. I was still longing for the simplicity and spiritual focus of the monastic life and decided to send off an expression of interest to a monastery where I had previously attended a retreat. I was also hoping to live in a community where I could collaborate with other contemplatives in recording our experiences in order to broaden the understanding of the inner journey. An old issue with sciatica flared up while I was waiting for a reply. Knowing that I would strive my utmost to contribute to the community, I was concerned that I would not be up to it. The reply being delayed due to unusual circumstances, together with the still debilitating sciatica, seemed like Divine intervention, and I concluded that it wasn't meant to be.

None of the treatments I tried had helped, and I was only able to join the bush walkers on shorter walks. My involvement with the choir continued. It gave me a focus and helped me not feel so isolated. Being a novice at reading music, I put a lot of time into preparing for performances. I also knitted each grandson a Fair Isle jumper (same pattern, different colours) to remind them of their Norwegian heritage. Before my father passed away (aged ninety-two), he had given me a copy of his genealogy, neatly handwritten and meticulously researched. He was able to trace one line of ancestors back to 1290, still in Norway, and he mentioned there were also predecessors who came from the Faeroe Islands (aka Fair Isles).

On one of my trips to Brisbane to visit family, I had asked Jasper if he had learned anything new at school and he replied, 'Not really.' His response gave me the idea of making a second 'Book of Life' to give to my grandsons. This book had a larger format and covered a range of topics including quantum physics, ancient archaeology, the chakra system and so on. Most importantly, I wanted to give them instructions in meditation and impart my understanding of the Divine Law. When Jasper had finished high school (Year 12), I gave him his book and he said: 'It's fantastic!'

***

Extracts from the *Book of Life II:*

MEDITATION
I sit — and I am aware of sitting.
I breathe — and I am aware of my breath.
I walk — and now I am aware that I walk.
I hear — and now I am paying attention to what I am hearing.

Feelings and thoughts arise and pass. Between two thoughts there is silence. Be aware of the space between thoughts.

The natural rhythm of activity and quiet can be likened to music. We cannot have music without rests. The silent pause between the notes creates the rhythm. The heartbeat is the natural drum. Rhythm is part of nature and our inner nature—the seasons of change. Meditation brings insight and self-knowledge. We cannot change what we are not aware of. What we are not conscious of will be played out in our dreams where our unconscious mind can safely act out our unmet needs and hidden agendas. Symbolism is used to reveal the truth and sometimes the most extraordinary plots and adventures are productions worthy of an Oscar! Dreams can even contain revelations and premonitions.
—Grandma Ree (Marie)

Set aside the many competing explanations of the Big Bang; something made an entire cosmos out of nothing. It is this realisation—that something

transcendent started it all— which has hard science types using terms like 'miracle.'
—*The Case for a Creator* by Lee Strobel

The evolution of morals has not occurred either through the exercise of reasoning or through experience. The crude struggle for existence draws into play those resources of the body and properties of the mind which help one to overcome other competitors and rivals in the race for survival.... But the moral virtues that have been highly regarded since the dawn of civilization and are admired even today are the very opposite of these traits.
—*Living with Kundalini* by Pandit Gopi Krishna

***

2012: 7 February

I woke up during the night (not from dreaming) in a very empty and dark inner place. It felt like the Divine inner light had suddenly been turned off. This was unlike anything I had ever experienced. I was certain I could not live like this and prayed 'God help me' ceaselessly. Thank God it lifted at dawn!

Being in the habit of observing my feelings, later that year, I noticed that the yearning to live in a monastic community had ceased. I concluded that the energy had run its course. The thought of writing a book had started to take form. Maybe I was meant to live in the world, isolated, but with time to write?

2013

After I told Patrick that I needed a computer to transfer the content of my diaries, he found me an ex-government computer and gave me a crash course in how to use it. I soon started the task of transcribing a suitcase full of notes and diaries. While I was creating a file for the mystical experiences, a pattern emerged. Whenever there was an attempt to speak about the encounter with the man in the lift (in 1973), something mysterious had happened: the wind phenomenon in 1978, the interruption by three knocks on the door in 1982 and 1997, as well as the drops in both Paul's and my eyes in 1990.

I have only had two experiences where my mind has been 'closed' (temporarily 'wiped')—once after the encounter with the man in the lift and again in 1975 after the encounter with the man in the snow. After he vanished, leaving no footprints, I walked home, and it was only when I put the key in my front door that I recalled this extraordinary event. I could now see that these two experiences were also connected by the symbol of the key, as the man in the lift was carrying an unusually large bundle of keys.

I now wondered whether the same spiritual being had also been responsible for other mystical experiences, such as the vision of the cross in the sky (1976) and the being that sat at the end of my bed 'stretching' my big toe (1980). (The big toe, according to Ayurvedic physicians, is connected to the brain, and the tip of the big toe corresponds to the pineal gland. In some Eastern religions, the pineal gland is said to be the seat of higher consciousness and clairvoyance.)

While doing the Divine Office, I started to write down texts that reminded me of my mystical experiences:

I was dead, and behold, I am alive and I hold the keys of death. (Rev. 1:18)
Behold, I stand at the door and knock, says the Lord. (Rev. 3:20)
…and you will see my back; but my face will not be seen. (Exodus 33:23)
He then opened their minds to understand the scriptures. (Luke 24:45)

2014

Amongst my diaries I found the psalm below handwritten on a photocopy of a photograph. I would have photocopied the photo in order to write the psalm beneath it. This photo was taken in Norway in the 1980s and depicts my mother and myself with an oil painting on the wall behind us. This is the only oil painting I have ever done. As a teenager, I had tried to copy a painting I found in one of my father's books at home. For some reason, the harvest scene, with a woman dressed in a black hooded robe carrying a bundle of sheaves, appealed to me.

Later in life, I was struck by how this painting and the psalm 'resembled' my spiritual journey. The black habit the woman is wearing reminded me of my monastic dream and of the meeting in the lift with the man in a black robe. This psalm reminded me of the years of 'mourning' that were necessary for spiritual transformation:

Deliver us, O Lord, from our bondage as streams in dry land. Those who are sowing in tears will sing when they reap. They go out, they go out, full of tears, carrying seed for the sowing: They come back, they come back, full of song, carrying their sheaves.
[photo 2] (Psalm 126)

I take an interest in the symbolic meaning of pastimes that people are passionate about. Years ago I liked doing crosswords. At that time, I was looking for explanations for what was happening to me during my spiritual process. It was after I found the explanation to my state that I switched to Sudoku (a puzzle requiring logic to fill in three-by-three grids of boxes with the numerals one through nine). In Sudoku, the numbers are given and they have a set place—which have to be found. Just as there are empty spaces to fill, I have an unfulfilled need to share what I know.

A friend once told me that someone had commented on her passion for doing quilting. The person asked my friend why she bothered cutting up material into pieces only to stitch them back together again! Knowing something about my friend's wounded past, I wondered if she was trying to stitch together pieces of herself that had been torn apart.

Patrick's love of rocks and gemstones goes back a long time. As a child he started fossicking when we were on camping holidays in the Flinders Ranges in South Australia. Crystals became his passion, and later, his livelihood. Recently he had begun to superimpose his photographs of crystals onto images of animals, mermaids, birds and planets. It was when I saw how the crystals permeated all his work that I asked myself: 'What is the symbolic meaning of crystals?'

I found these quotes:

...The Saint is like the clear, well-cut crystal which, being without any stains fully absorbs all the rays of light and sends them out again, intensified by its concentrative power. Unable are the rays to stain the crystal by their various colours. They cannot pierce its hardness, nor disturb its harmonious structure. Unchanged remains the crystal in its genuine purity and strength.
—*The Four Sublime States* (Buddhist publication)

Truth cannot be found by clinging to anything within the phenomenal world; the foundation of consciousness is deeper than any phenomenal perception... (Commentary on the Diamond Sutra)

'Cryst-al' made me think of 'Christ in all' from a Christian perspective:

Christ yesterday and Christ today
For all eternity the same,
The image of our hidden God;
Eternal wisdom is his name.
—Hymn from the Divine Office

In 2013, I wrote this poem for Patrick:
Crystal forming in the dark
Luminous, transparent when uncovered...

Since I started transcribing my notes and diaries, the dreams of being alone and lost in the city at night have ceased. I cannot remember having dreamt anything for a long time.

When I am on my own, my inner state of tranquillity is energetically neutral. As soon as I interact with others, such as a chance meeting in the street, there is a subtle but vibrant feeling of pure joy. When I engage in idle small talk, it results in me feeling 'drained.' Interacting with others often involves talking about the past or the future, to which I cannot emotionally relate. Sometimes when I have a conversation about God or the Divine, a sacred presence is felt making us lower our voices in reverence.

Praying for others is meaningful. I start each prayer with: 'In the name of the Father and of the Son and of the Holy Spirit, and blessed Virgin Mary and all the angels and saints.' I thank God for the Peace that has been bestowed on me and for guidance to serve where I have something to offer. I never think of myself as pure. Pure Awareness is not about me, it is only to the extent that I am empty that I feel and know the Sacred essence.

> *For our Lord bestows His blessings where he finds vessels empty to receive them. And the more completely a man renounces worldly things and the more perfectly he dies to self by the conquest of self, the sooner will Grace be given, the more richly will it be infused, and the nearer to God will it raise the heart set free from the world.*
> *—The Imitation of Christ* by Thomas à Kempis

2015

In May, I noticed a sizeable lump in my breast. I had not been to a doctor for over seven years and was not registered as a patient anywhere. (I had not needed a prescription either before or since I took hormone replacement for extreme hot flushes.) When I found a GP, I was sent for a series of tests that warranted a biopsy. On the morning that I was to have the tests, I was given a vision.

2015: 29 May

Upon waking at dawn, with eyes still closed: I find myself looking at an image, some distance away, of a man standing with outstretched arms in the opening of a grotto (stone cave). It is dark inside the grotto, but the cross-shaped figure is made visible by the bright light surrounding him. I do not take my eyes off him but become aware of what appears to be a scene of heaven above the grotto. The sky around this scene is black. The Christ figure suddenly starts moving and walks out of the grotto towards me. The images fade, then disappear.

It was clear to me that this inner vision was a Divine gift and not a product of my own mind. I understood the vision to be the risen Christ entering the world.

The results of the biopsy revealed I had an aggressive cancer. Before I could even decide on a date for the surgery, a prospective buyer turned up. The house had been on the market for over two years, and this was the second time I had tried to sell. I was gardening when the real estate agent came outside and said: 'You have a sale!' The couple were delighted with the property and did not even want to bargain.

Paul came to help me pack and take me to medical appointments, which was a great help. I postponed treatment options because I was about to move. A quick decision was made to put an offer in for a unit in the same complex where

Paul lived. That unit had also been for sale for a long time, and I was fortunate to buy it at a price I could afford. It all felt like Divine providence. Neither the unexpected news of cancer nor the move to a different environment had any impact on my state of inner peace.

Lismore

At the end of July 2015, I moved back to Lismore. After consultations with my new oncologist, I agreed to have a lumpectomy. It was fortunate that I was able to stay with Paul while I was recovering from surgery and my unit was being renovated. When my doctor informed me that the margin was clear, I decided that unless there were signs the cancer had spread, I didn't want any further treatment, as it would interfere with my writing.

2016

In February, Gini accepted my invitation to edit my book draft. In the past, Gini and I had worked together on articles for the SEN journals, which we had edited over the phone. Now that we were both living in the Lismore area, Gini offered to come to my place for weekly editing, as I don't drive. Whenever I doubted my capacity to complete this project, I was reassured by her ongoing commitment. Recognising the need for a narrative, she asked me to make the story more personal and therefore more engaging for the reader. This was a new thought for me. Admittedly, the mystical experiences and the process of spiritual transformation did not happen in isolation but in the here and now of family life. Making my personal life public was challenging as I am a private person and am also concerned for the privacy of others. Fortunately, Paul has been supportive of my writing, as has my immediate family.

2017

I live in a strata complex of nine duplexes occupied by sixteen mainly elderly women. I joined the strata committee not long after I had moved into my unit. I felt ready to participate, as my ability to concentrate had improved over time. It is good to have something to offer and also be able to contribute in other areas of communal living on a more personal and practical level.

Although writing has never come easily to me, I make an effort to engage with the media whenever I feel prompted to speak up, usually concerning spiritual matters. The following letter was printed in a Catholic newspaper in October. The paper had a weekly column titled 'Can you change a life? – AskOne': *Can you make a difference in the life of one Catholic who is no longer involved in the life of the Church? All it takes is for you to AskOne person to come back to Mass regularly.*

> My reply was: *Listening to why people stop going to church can also make a difference. When I asked some so-called 'lapsed' Catholic friends the reason why they had stopped going to church, one said she was hurt and disillusioned by the behaviour of clergy. After listening to some of her personal experiences I looked her in the eyes and told her she hadn't lapsed—it was the church that had failed her. After hearing that,*

tears rolled down her face. 'I lost faith in the Church but I still believe in God and pray,' she said.

Another Catholic friend told me that her mother used to take her and her sisters to Mass every week. Due to the fact that her parents were not married (her father was a divorcee), her mother had suffered greatly under the stigma attached to that. My friend said she always felt like an illegitimate child and as a teenager was relieved to leave the church for good. I thanked her for telling me her story and validated her feelings. It still hurts, she said— a woman in her sixties whose deep wounds are still raw.

2017: 7 September

An inner vision: Upon waking at dawn, with eyes still closed, I see a straight dirt road leading to a tree at the top of a hill. The road is obstructed by large rocks, but I can see there is a narrow path in between the three rocks. The tree is symmetrically shaped, and this makes me think of 'the tree of life.'

The only other time I have had this kind of inner vision was when I saw a Christlike figure walking out of a grotto in 2015. Both these images were unusually clear and bright, and both disappeared as soon as I had 'interpreted' what I saw.

2017: 14 September

I was reading the Divine Office (as I do every morning), and the day's reading was 'The Exaltation of The Holy Cross' (Feast

Day of 14 September). I was reminded of my two visions when I read:

Ant. 1: After he had been crucified he rose from the dead and brought us redemption, alleluia.

Ant. 2: In the centre of the holy city of Jerusalem stands the tree of life, and the leaves of that tree will bring salvation to all peoples, alleluia.

(Antiphon: a versicle, said or chanted, before and after a psalm or hymn, varying with the church season and feast.)

I wrote these antiphons down in my diary because of the similarities to my visions and the sequence of the resurrection and the tree of life. In my ignorance, I did not know what 'the tree of life' symbolised. When I was checking to see if what I had written down was accurate, I discovered that these antiphons were in fact in Evening prayer 1 for 13 September. I now got to read the Morning prayer of 14 September and it was this hymn:

O Cross of Christ, immortal tree
On which our Saviour died,
The world is sheltered by your arms
That bore the Crucified.
From bitter death and barren wood
The tree of life is made;
Its branches bear unfailing fruit
And leaves that never fade.
—Hymn from the Divine Office

The goal of the quest ....is often called Jerusalem by the Christian mystics: naturally enough, since that city was for the mediaeval mind the supreme end of pilgrimage.
— *Mysticism. The Development of Humankind's Spiritual Consciousness* by Evelyn Underhill

2017: 30 September

During the night, I woke up gasping for air. I noticed the 'electric' tingling sensation throughout the whole body was a lot stronger than usual, especially in the lower legs and soles of the feet. The headache disappeared when I got up, but I felt lightheaded and was also short of breath. Unsure if this was symptomatic of the increased 'charge,' a heart attack or both, I decided the sensible thing to do was to unlock the front door and pack a bag for hospital. There was no change to my inner state of peace while all this was going on.

In the morning, breathing was back to normal. I later had a checkup with my GP, which showed that my health was okay. Wanting to see if this condition could be related to spiritual transformation, I looked in Solomae Sananda's book *Kundalini and the Evolution of Consciousness*. I had used this book in the past as a reference for symptoms of an active Kundalini.

The following quotes are from a list of signs and symptoms:

– Changes in breathing patterns or the cessation of breathing all together, especially during meditation.

– When there is a large increase in prana through the system, there can be a momentary slowing down or

cutting off of oxygen to the brain.... This can result in a fainting spell or feelings of light-headedness or dizziness, as occurs when you hold your breath for an extended period.

I wondered if what happened to me that night could be described as 'a large increase in prana.'

2018: 4 February

Doing the Divine Office in the morning, I read in the Psalter: *The gates of heaven were opened to Christ because he was lifted up in the flesh.* (St Irenaeus)

Being 'lifted up' reminded me of the meeting with the mysterious man in the lift. While that fleeting thought went through my mind, I suddenly became aware of tears gently flowing down my face. I was not sad. I felt touched by Grace...

Around Easter, I noticed an amplification of the 'brightness' and 'charge' in the brain and the tingling sensation felt stronger—more concentrated. Increases in Divine Light sensitise the nervous system, and there is an ongoing need for solitude and silence. It suits me best to live on my own, but Paul lives close by and we meet up most days. Fortunately he drives, enabling us to go for walks in the forest and on the beach. Despite the challenges of our relationship, there is still a deep and abiding love between us.

In August, I wrote a letter to St. Benedict's Monastery asking permission to use the quotes from Father Thomas Keating's books. I also included the Acknowledgments page from this book. It was good timing. I got a reply from his assistant who was leaving shortly to travel interstate to visit him at St. Joseph's Abbey. This is where he had been the abbot some decades ago and where they had an infirmary where he was being cared for. On 25 October 2018, Father Thomas Keating died at the age of ninety-five. On hearing the news, there was a subtle sadness and a sense of his absence in this worldly sphere. And at the same time, there is Grace…

In the state of Pure Awareness, nothing lingers on. Momentarily there can be sadness or joy, but these feelings soon vanish into the vast expanse of equanimity. These are moments that cannot be relived. Memories and thoughts do not produce any feelings or emotions. In the Now, there is no 'space' or 'time' to experience a reaction to past or future events. Being unemotional and unattached is not the same as being indifferent. The source of Pure Love makes me respond spontaneously to a person's need and contribute where I have something to offer, without being motivated by a sense of obligation or a need for acknowledgment. The sacred essence is always present, yet I feel ordinary and am aware of my shortcomings.

Absorbed in silent prayer, I gaze at this mystery which I cannot describe because it is not separate from me—it cannot be reflected on.
God, as the Beloved, is the mystery which I worship
and which is worshipping in me.
And at the same time
God is who and that which I humbly serve…

****

A Contemplative Mystic

1

2

Marie Gundersen

3

4

A Contemplative Mystic

5

6

7

8

Postscript

'The Book of Life' is being written while we are editing the past...
In February 2019, I decided to have a consultation with Lena McGregor, the clairvoyant healer, about a breathing issue I had first noticed in September last year. The X-ray taken at the time showed nothing abnormal. The symptoms of wheezy breathing (called stridor) and soreness in the upper solar plexus area were not getting better and warranted another X-ray. This was interpreted by the radiologist to be COPD—chronic obstructive pulmonary disease—possibly emphysema.

When I saw Lena, I didn't tell her the result of this X-ray. I asked her to examine my chest area carefully. She said she could see a dark spot over my right upper chest. On the next visit a few weeks later, when I asked her to have a closer look at this area, she found that the original spot was larger and could also see cancer in the sternum. Without her assessment, I would not have gone to my GP to ask for a CT scan of my chest.

This revealed that I had cancer in the right lung, a bronchogenic carcinoma with lymph node spread. There was no sign of cancer in the bones, but a PET scan was recommended for more clarity. Thanks to Lena and the timing of this consultation, I did find out I have cancer. In March I had a lung biopsy that showed the cancer was a metastasised breast cancer. There was no reaction in me to the news that I had advanced cancer—my inner state hadn't changed. I was interested to hear that Lena saw no sign of cancer in my 'spiritual body.'

Lena described it this way: 'When Marie initially came to me with discomfort in her chest and breathing difficulties, I measured her chakras, which is one of the diagnostic tools. When I did this, the chakras were all stable and quite big considering what I found in the energy body and what Marie was experiencing. This matched with Marie's experience of not being affected emotionally or mentally by her physical condition and showed a spiritual stability and a true blessing of grace.'

Since the cancer diagnosis, Paul has come with me to all medical appointments, and we are spending more time together. Shortness of breath, due to cancer, is increasingly restricting my activities. The focus now, is getting my manuscript ready for publication. My computer is not connected to the internet. Fortunately, Paul is assisting me with emails. I feel blessed to have his support and that we can continue to share the journey through the unfamiliar 'landscape' of living with a terminal illness.

2019: 15 April

After a late consultation with the oncologist (where it was decided that I would be referred to a palliative doctor), Paul and I were walking home in the dark. Paul was behind me on the path leading to my unit when we noticed a blue butterfly encircling us. With key in hand, I walked towards the entrance. The blue butterfly kept hovering close to me, clearly visible under the lamplight above the door. I have never before seen a blue butterfly in my little garden. And its unusual appearance at this time seemed symbolic.

Reflections on the Journey

I started writing a journal in 1973 after the meeting with the mysterious man in the lift. It was only later that I understood the significance of the seven floors we ascended together—I learnt that the Kundalini force moves through the seven major chakras. The mysterious capitalising of 'FROM THE GROUND FLOOR TO THE SEVENTH FLOOR' (2007) convinced me that I was being given a message: to revive the knowledge of the link between spiritual transformation and the chakra system.

Here are some multicultural references to the serpent power or Kundalini, which can be found in *Emergence,* vol. 4, no. 2 (2000):

-Kundalini is a Sanskrit word meaning 'coiled up' like a snake or spring charged with latent energy or power. It refers to the energy that rises along the spine in the process of spiritual awakening, working through the egoistic obstructions to our final Self-realisation.

-In the Jewish Kabbalah the serpent is a re-creation of all that is and all that is not. In the Bible's book of Genesis the mission of the serpent in the Garden of Eden is to plunge Adam and Eve into evolution.

-Carl Jung, the eminent Swiss psychoanalyst, gave a seminar on Kundalini. Jung contended that the beast (dragon) is the symbol of the Kundalini, the force that, in psychological terms, obliges a person to go on his or her greatest adventure—the adventure of self-knowledge.

-Itzahak Bentov, an American biomedical engineer, investigated Kundalini awakening and developed a physiological model of it.... A harmoniously pulsating magnetic field around the head seems to be one of the results of an awakened Kundalini. Bentov's colleague, Dr. Sannella, reached a conclusion about Kundalini saying the idea of spiritual rebirth or enlightenment has become a definite, well-defined clinical entity.

In Christianity, too, there are references to the spiritual serpent energy (Kundalini):

In Naassene Christianity, the Divine Mother dispenses herself in the form of a very special grace, the Holy Spirit, which she bestows from above, bringing about the spontaneous awakening of the latent spiritual (or serpent) energy in the disciple, which the Naassenes associated with the reversal of the flow. Within the context of Naassene Christianity, then, the serpent was a symbol for this ineffable spiritual energy.
—Gnostic Secrets of the Naassenes
by Mark H. Gaffney

There is suffering in spiritual transformation just as in childbirth: a new being conceived by the union of male and female energies grows and develops in the darkness of the womb. The contractions in labour intensify just before birth. Then there is a sudden ending of pain as the infant emerges into light ready for a new stage of development. It is said that the polarities of the male (positive) and female (negative) energies are merged through the Kundalini process.

In 1987, I was told by an inner voice: 'You will be turned inside out.' This was a forewarning of the transformation about to affect me on a cellular level. Heart palpitations and anxiety attacks were related to changes in the electrical impulses most likely caused by years of intense meditation practice.

> *Kundalini is fundamentally associated with the spiritualzing of body and mind, expanding the capacity of the human to experience and hold the infinite. It is a slow development, as all evolutionary changes are slow. It is often painful both physically and psychologically as it involves both dissolution of blocks to expansion and the giving up of identity, beliefs, and attachments.*
> —*Energies of Transformation. A Guide to the Kundalini Process* by Bonnie Greenwell

Kundalini is still largely unknown to the general public and the medical profession. I think a better understanding of this primal force may in time bridge the gap between different scientific modalities and even provide the missing link between science and religion. Clairvoyantly, the chakras (Sanskrit for 'wheels') are perceived as vortices of coloured light.

A clairvoyant person would have much to offer given more opportunities for collaboration.

Research of the Kundalini process has been going on for many years, but less understood is the relationship between the Kundalini energy and the Holy Spirit. Solomae Sananda, in *Kundalini and the Evolution of Consciousness*, offers a possible explanation:

> *Kundalini represents the ascent of matter into spirit.... The Holy Spirit represents the descent of spirit into matter. ... The Western paradigm (Christianity) focuses mainly on the Divine energy as the Holy Spirit, not recognizing the Kundalini energy as the force that purifies the lower nature, thus making it possible to be united with the Divine self while in a physical body.*

In 1975, as I was stepping across the threshold into my bedroom, I experienced an inner calling and made a 'mystical vow.' Years later, I was given a book on the anthroposophical teachings of Rudolf Steiner and found references to the threshold, which reminded me of my life-changing experience. In short, I learned that 'the threshold' is the boundary between the inner and outer world and that there are two guardians of the threshold. The lesser guardian is concerned with the inward journey—'to know yourself'— and the greater guardian represents 'the path towards the redemption of the world.' These 'encounters' could be described as initiations. The guardian experiences 'occur in many forms, often unexpectedly.'

Extracts from *Man on the Threshold* by Bernard Lievegoed:

In the Middle Ages, in post-Christian times, the mystics were no longer guided by a living guru. They could go their path permeating themselves with Christ. [Christ the teacher within.] When modern man suddenly crosses the threshold ... he knows how imperfect he is, but at the same time has acquired the everlasting power to keep striving for perfection under all circumstances of life...

In 1981, I received another important message: *Fear is overcome only when it is experienced to its very limits.* (This is encapsulated in the teachings of J. Krishnamurti, which I had not yet encountered.) Immediately after this prophetic message was delivered, I travelled through a dark 'tunnel' where I watched grazing sheep with glowing, red-hot bodies. I was amazed at their serenity. On reflection, the dark tunnel symbolises the Dark Night—the stage of annihilation. And the image of the red-hot sheep connects the transformational inner fire with the sacrificial lamb (Jesus Christ). I found references to the Lamb when I started reading the Divine Office: *Worthy is the Lamb who was slain to receive power and divinity, and wisdom and strength and honour, alleluia.* (Apoc. 5:12)

I am the good shepherd, says the Lord; I know my sheep and mine know me, just as the Father knows me and I know the Father; and I lay down my life for my sheep. (John 10:14–15)

*He who gave for us his life,
who for us endured the strife,*

Is our Pascal Lamb today!
We too sing for joy, and say
He who bore all pain and loss
Comfortless upon the Cross,
Lives in glory now on high,
Pleads for us, and hears our cry.
—Hymn from the Divine Office

In 1982, not long after this visionary experience, I was introduced to Krishnamurti's teachings and began practising meditation in daily life. A fundamental theme in Krishnamurti's teachings is the reality that the outer world is an expression of our inner state of mind, and if we want to change existing conditions, we must first transform ourselves. This involves becoming aware of our desires and attachments and also how we identify with our ideas and opinions (our conditioning). He said that it is awareness that liberates the mind, not the conformity to ideas:

> *When you give your complete attention—I mean with everything in you—there is no observer at all.... That total silence in which there is neither the observer nor the thing observed is the highest form of a religious mind. ... In that silence there is a state of energy in which there is no conflict. (Freedom from the Known* by J. Krishnamurti)

There are references in scripture that point to the need to silence the mind for spiritual transformation to take place but do not address how that happens:

Be still and know that I am God. (Psalm 46)

Adapt yourselves no longer to the pattern of this present world, but let your minds be remade and your whole nature thus transformed. Then you will be able to discern the will of God, and to know what is good, acceptable, and perfect. (Rom. 12:1–2)

It was in Krishnamurti's teaching that I learned how to 'remake my mind.' Krishnamurti maintained that truth is everywhere and in everything, and it reveals its very nature if we observe carefully from moment to moment:

Take a bud, an actual bud from a bush. If you nip it, it will never flower, it will die quickly. If you let it blossom, then it shows you the colour, the delicacy, the pollen, everything. (Krishnamurti on Education)

Krishnamurti uses jealousy as an example of an emotion flowering and dying:

In the same way, if you allow jealousy to flower, then it shows you everything it actually is—which is envy, attachment. So in allowing jealousy to blossom, it has shown you all its colours and it has revealed to you what is behind jealousy, which you will never discover if you do not allow it to blossom. ... You let the fact flower and it opens other doors, till there is no flowering at all of any kind.
—*Krishnamurti on Education*

When I discovered Father Thomas Keating's teachings, I found there was a Christian practice leading to the same outcome Krishnamurti was describing:

> *Our unconscious, prerational emotional programming from childhood and our over-identification with a specific group or groups are the sources from which our false self—our injured, compensatory sense of who we are—gradually emerges and stabilizes... the gift of contemplative prayer is a practical and essential tool for confronting the heart of the Christian ascesis—namely, the struggle with our unconscious motivation—while at the same time establishing the climate and necessary dispositions for a deepening relationship with God and leading, if we persevere, to divine union.*
> —*Invitation to Love. The Way of Christian Contemplation* by Thomas Keating

According to Krishnamurti, attention is like a flame that can burn away the wounds of being hurt and anything that is unresolved. He also suggests that it is the 'shock of attention' that alters the stimulus-response patterns and the established circuits of brain activity, eventually causing the dissolution of the self. The effects of the 'flame of focused attention,' it seems to me, could also be described as purification by the Divine Light—the Light that purges, purifies, illuminates and sanctifies.

In his teachings, Krishnamurti did not elaborate on his process of transformation. It was in two volumes of biography that I found a more detailed description of how meditation had affected him:

I woke at three with a sense of extraordinary fire, light burning in the mind. There was no observer. The testing was from the outside but the observer didn't exist. There was only that and nothing else. The power penetrated the whole being. I sat up and it lasted three hours.
—*Krishnamurti: The Open Door* by Mary Lutyens

Some years later, Krishnamurti tries to describe another experience of transformational energy:

Krishnamurti had had 'peculiar meditations' which were 'unpremeditated and grew with intensity,' and one night he 'woke up to find something totally different and new. The movement had reached the source of all energy. ... One may ask with what assurance do you state that it is the source of all energy? One can only reply with complete humility that it is so. ... After the body had somewhat rested, there was the perception that there was nothing beyond this.'
—*Krishnamurti: The Open Door* by Mary Lutyens

In another volume of biography by Mary Lutyens, *J. Krishnamurti: The Years of Awakening*, I read that Krishnamurti endured both physical and mental agonies. What stood out for me was this sentence: '...there is a loneliness, that of a solitary pine in the wilderness.'

During the night of 24 October 1990 an unknown force entered my body and 'hollowed' me out. The observer and the observed had merged, and there was an ending of time and my emotional connection with God and the world.

Looking at Christ hanging on the cross gave me some solace during the subsequent years of suffering annihilation—there is no resurrection without crucifixion. The following scripture reading implies that 'crucifixion' is an inner process necessary for transformation:

> *As for me, the only thing I can boast about is the cross of our Lord Jesus Christ, through whom the world is crucified to me, and I to the world. It does not matter if the person is circumcised or not; what matters is for him to become an altogether new creature.*
> (St. Paul's letter to the Galatians 6:14–15)

Jesus on the cross calls: *My God, my God, why have you forsaken me?'* (Mark 15:34) and *'Father, into your hands I commend my spirit.' With these words he breathed his last.* (Luke 23:46)

I am reminded about my dream in which a man announced that my pulse had stopped and I drew my last breath. Seven days later, on 17 December 1999, the force was reversed and I was released from the 'tomb.' A new stage and a new state of being—still imperfect and flawed but opened to receive Divine Light.

In 2003 when I 'misspelled' my name as Mary, I was not familiar with the parable of Martha and Mary. This parable highlights the qualities of the contemplative life. Jesus says, 'Mary has chosen what is better, and it will not be taken away from her.' (Luke 10:42)

My interest in Catholicism had been sparked by the teachings of the mystics, St. John of the Cross and St.

Teresa of Ávila. Their teachings resonated with my own understanding. When I realised that the expression the 'Dark Night of the Soul' was often misinterpreted, I felt compelled to write my article 'St. John of the Cross and the Dark Night of the Soul.' A professor of theology, after reading this article, said it was the best interpretation of St. John of the Cross he had read. His acknowledgement indirectly helped to validate my own spirituality.

Over the years, I gave my article on St. John of the Cross to parishioners, priests and even bishops but never received any feedback. Had they shown an interest in the mystics of the past, I would have shared more of my own spiritual journey. In conversation, I introduced them to the work of Father Thomas Keating and expressed the need for a revival of contemplative practices. The lack of interest shown contributed to my feeling estranged from the church. I would have liked to have something to offer and to be part of the parish community, but instead I remained an outsider.

I agree with Cynthia Bourgeault when she writes: *...the church's biggest institutional failure has been its incapacity to build the bridge between 'Martha and Mary' from (active life) external observances to conscious interiority (self-reflective level) to contemplative living...* (*The Heart of Centering Prayer: Nondual Christianity in Theory and Practice* by Cynthia Bourgeault)

Scripture and religious rituals have both an outer (exoteric) and an inner (esoteric) meaning. The esoteric, mystical dimension, encompassing the chakra system and process of transformation, is not taught by the church but is alluded to in scripture. Here are some examples:

1. Jesus said to Nicodemus: 'Do not be surprised when I say: You must be born from above. The wind blows wherever it pleases; you hear its sound, but you cannot tell where it comes from or where it is going. That is how it is with all who are born of the Spirit.' (John 3:7–8)

2. How blessed are the poor in spirit: the kingdom of Heaven is theirs. (Matthew 5:3)

3. If therefore thine eye be single, thy whole body shall be filled with light. (Matthew 6:22)

4. Sinless Eve, triumphant sign; Thou art she who crushed the serpent, Mary pledge of life divine. (Hymn from the Divine Office)

5. No one has gone up to heaven except the one who came down from heaven, the Son of man; as Moses lifted up the snake in the desert, so must the Son of man be lifted up so that everyone who believes may have eternal life in him. (John 3:13–15)

6. Having risen in the morning on the first day of the week, he appeared first to Mary of Magdala from whom he had cast out seven devils. ... After this, he showed himself under another form to two of them as they were on their way into the country. (Mark 16:9–12)

I wonder if something got lost in translation—is there a link here between the 'seven devils' and the serpent and Kundalini rising through the seven chakras? Is Mary Magdalene the *enlightened* apostle?

> *At the Savior's departure, Mary takes over his role. She comforts the distressed disciples, turns their hearts toward thoughts about the Savior's words, and gives them special teaching that will allow them to overcome the sin of the world. (Gospel of Mary 10:7–9) ... for centuries, the Gospel of Mary remained completely unknown. Only three fragmentary manuscripts are known to have survived into the modern period, two third-century Greek fragments and a longer fifth-century Coptic translation... (The Complete Gospels by Robert J. Miller)*

A REFORMATION, NO LESS, IS NEEDED IN REVIVING AND EXPLAINING THE CONTEMPLATIVE DIMENSION OF SCRIPTURE.

I first wrote this sentence in ordinary font but then deleted it and used 'Caps Lock,' as it seemed important to make it stand out from the ordinary text. When the sentence turned out in red, both on the screen and in print, I was surprised. Never before has the capitalising of a word or sentence appeared in red on my computer. Even if it is technically possible, I would not know how to do that.

When I pray the Divine Office, I use The Daily Prayer Book and the two St. Paul's Missals. In all three books, the headings are printed in red. After I had written the sentence that 'appeared' in red, I wondered if this was another mystical revelation with a message to the world...

In the Lord's Prayer in Aramaic, 'Hallowed be thy name' translates to: *Help us breathe one holy breath feeling only you— this creates a shrine inside, in wholeness. Help us let go, clear the space inside of busy forgetfulness: so the Name comes to live...* (*Prayers of the Cosmos. Meditations on the Aramaic words of Jesus* by Neil Douglas- Klotz)

Evelyn Underhill has a deep understanding of the mystical path. Here is an extract from a thick but very readable book entitled *Mysticism. The Development of Humankind's Spiritual Consciousness*:

> *The self has got to learn to cease to be its 'own centre and circumference': to make that final surrender which is the price of final peace. In the Dark Night the starved and tortured spirit learns through an anguish which is 'itself an orison' to accept lovelessness for the sake of Love, Nothingness for the sake of the All; dies without any sure promise of life, loses when it hardly hopes to find. ... Only when the journey to God is completed begins the 'Journey in God'—that which the Christian mystics call the Unitive Way—and this, since it is the essence of Eternal Life, can have no end.... The mystic says: 'Nought I am, nought I have, nought I lack.'*

Union with God is not a conversion experience. Union implies the absence of a separate self—it is not an experience because there is no 'experiencer.' Pure Awareness or Pure

Subjectivity is seeing without the split of the Seer and the Seen—a state which cannot be reflected on. Living in the Now is a timeless state where there is no Self-reflection, no personal satisfactions. All is Grace…

> *Sufi teacher Hidayat Inayat Khan says, In the heart there is only place for one: either the self or the Beloved.… The whole striving of the mystic is not only to raise one's own consciousness to higher spheres, but also help others in the same process.*

In *The Better Part, Stages of Contemplative Living*, Father Thomas Keating writes:

> *To be in dialogue with the other world religions requires the contemplative experience because all in their fully developed spiritual disciplines have experienced it. This fact suggests that the members of the other world religions must henceforth be fully accepted as brothers and sisters, greatly loved by God and blessed with resources of immense value to contribute to us and to the world at large. The great gift that contemplative persons offer is the experience of the divine presence. Who is going to bring this realization into society if not those who are experiencing it?*

Divine Law

For the Spirit of God fills the whole universe and holds all things together. (Wisdom 1:7)

God is that which is unchangeable, ever present, whole and Holy. The phenomenal world is changeable. Spiritually, the soul is always connected to God the source of Love—whilst physically we live in a world of change and decay. We spend our lives pursuing a happiness that is illusory—it does not last. There is something deeper in us, our soul, which yearns for that which is permanent, not transient. What prompts us on the journey of self-knowledge is ultimately the yearning to know God. What fires our desire is the need to experience wholeness in love. Any attachment to finite things is an impurity that prevents complete union with God who is infinite love.

It is the Divine Light that purges (empties) and purifies and in so doing enlightens us. With the inflow of Divine Light, I notice that thoughts entering my mind are highlighted and an assessment of these thoughts happens instantly. It is clear to me that this 'inner judgement' is not done by a personal critic but by the Divine Light. I welcome these 'exposures' because in my heart they feel right and just—confession and communion takes place within. The presence and action of this inner Light affirms to me the Divine Law.

In the scroll of the book it stands written that I should do your will. My God, I delight in your law in the depth of my heart. (Psalm 39)

Divine Law is imprinted in our spiritual heart and speaks to us through our conscience. Our rational and conditioned mind usually speaks with a louder voice. Discerning what we are hearing and who we are listening to requires awareness. This is a spiritual practice. Meditation increases awareness and self-knowledge. With more awareness we can cease to be dominated by our instinctual drives for survival and control, thus transcending the lower chakras. Self-centred gratification and poor impulse control do not lead to inner peace and harmonious living.

The notion that there is a law governing human nature is ancient. Among the many philosophers who adhered to this concept of a natural law inherent in human nature was Cicero (106–143 BCE) who wrote: 'What is right and true is also eternal and does not begin or end with written statutes.' Nature reflects the Divine Law—'as above, so below.'

In our modern times, many human rights are protected by the United Nations Universal Declaration of Human Rights. Protection of human rights and the concept of crimes against humanity are based on this natural law. A democratic system of governance is not sufficient without a foundation based on the Divine Law. Without the need to protect ourselves from the enemy, countries could save the enormous amounts spent on armament and redirect this money to shelter, food, education and healthcare for all.

Modern society is controlled by forces that overstimulate the senses in young persons. Intellectual knowledge is highly prized and marketing encourages spending beyond our needs and capacity to pay. Spiritual teaching would give students a wider horizon and a map of the Way—the soul's journey.

The practice of meditation and contemplation is a journey into stillness and could be an integral part of the curriculum in schools and higher education.

Speak Lord, your servant is listening. (1 Samuel 3:10)

The world needs to rediscover the Divine Law, which is governing each of us. This is crucial for our inner development and peaceful coexistence.

Appendix A

Copies of some of my correspondence with Father Thomas Keating:

Valla Beach, 14 Sept. 2010
Dear Fr. Thomas Keating

Thank you so much for your invaluable contributions to the contemplative life!
A couple of years ago I came across an ebook called 'Kundalini Energy and Christian Spirituality' by Philip St. Romain. In the foreword you say: *This book will initiate Christians on the spiritual journey into this important but long neglected dimension of the transforming power of grace.*
I am grateful for this quote, which together with the writing helped to place aspects of my own inner process in a Christian context. The world at large needs to rediscover and redefine the spiritual dimension; to inform science, education, politics and religion etc. I sense a certain urgency to respond to this need and wonder if in collaboration with others, my own story and experiences may be useful? I am a retired woman in my sixties who started journaling in 1973 detailing experiences, states and stages related to my process.

The article: 'A Modern Mystic' printed in this SEN journal is a short summary of this ongoing spiritual journey. I was also prompted to write the article on: 'St. John of the Cross and the Dark Night of the Soul.' The Dark Night of the Soul is often 'pathologised' and the expression misused because there is a lack of understanding the spiritual dimension; the paradox of suffering—the Way of the Cross...

Aware of your age and demand on your time, I shall not expect a personal reply, but will be delighted to know if you have received and read these articles.

Peace be with you... Marie Gundersen

***

A Contemplative Mystic

SAINT BENEDICT'S MONASTERY
CISTERCIAN monks

October 26, 2010

Marie Gunderson
31 / 1 Regatta Drive
Valla Beach, NSW 2448
AUSTRALIA

Dear Marie,

I received and have read your articles and encourage you to consider sharing more of your experience for the very reasons you give in your letter. Anyone overtaken by the awakening of kundalini will be interested in hearing your Christian experience of it.

Perhaps you will feel inspired to enlarge on these two articles or use them as a basis for a book with a lot more details. Those you have shared are very helpful and well written.

In Christ's love,

Thomas Keating

Valla Beach, 12 Nov. 2010
Dear Fr. Thomas Keating,

I felt very blessed to receive your letter of reply (26 Oct.)— thank you so much! This has encouraged me to start transcribing my notes onto disc with the intention God willing, to try and find an editor/publisher at some stage.
Peace be with you ... Marie Gundersen

***

Valla Beach, 9 Jan. 2013
Dear Fr. Thomas Keating,

Thank you for the beautifully presented book: *Heartfulness. Transformation in Christ.*
I found this book both inspiring and thought provoking. Reading Chapter 5 on Suffering made me stop to ponder the two very different faces of the Buddha and Christ and how they relate to our own spiritual process.
I once asked the question: 'Does a Buddhist need Christ?' And the answer was: 'The Buddha was called but Jesus Christ was sent. Buddha sought Enlightenment. Christ was the Light (the Enlightened one).'
I, the Light, have come into the world. (Jn. 12:46)
This difference made me wonder if Buddha and Christ represent two stages of the spiritual process: Buddha describing the path to Enlightenment and Christ guiding us beyond Enlightenment? Enlightenment is sometimes described as a blissful detachment to the illusionary nature of the world. It is also said that Enlightenment deepens, so maybe one is on a mental level, the other a deeper transformation on a cellular level?

My own experience is that I knew a blissful state before years of practising mindfulness led to a sudden shift of awareness into the present moment; an ending of time. This shift into the centre closed the 'gap' between subject and object. Physically it was felt like a compression and mentally there was no self-reflective movement and 'space' for any emotional feedback (which operates in time), including the emotion of God's love (love as my emotional connection with God). Deep feelings of annihilation and abandonment lasted for years. Looking at Christ's face of agony gave some solace and hope.
The outcome (as I described in the SEN journal posted to you earlier) was like a rebirth; a new body, still imperfect and flawed, but filled with light and a sacred, subtle presence of love... Not an emotional feeling.
Jesus on the cross calls: *Father, why hast Thou forsaken us?* and *Father, into Thy hand I yield back my spirit.*
When we are asked to follow Christ to the Cross we are asked to die to the world and surrender to God. Feelings of abandonment and horrendous agony may not be caused by our deliberate separation from God, but rather suffering through a painful process of rebirth sustained by the love of God...? Now I am soul and have a body, not the other way around. A transformation process of death...
I have been crucified with Christ and yet I am alive; yet it is no longer I, but Christ living in me. (Gal. 2:20)
I wish you all the best, and thank you for educating, illuminating, inspiring and challenging me with your writings!
I apologise for my lack of English proficiency.
Any comments will be greatly appreciated.
God Bless you, Marie Gundersen

Marie Gundersen

SAINT BENEDICT'S MONASTERY
CISTERCIAN monks

February 5, 2013

M. Gundersen
31/1 Regatta Drive
Valla Beach, NSW 2480
AUSTRALIA

Dear Marie,

You seem to be well guided by the Spirit. I don't have much to suggest for your reflection. The image of the two faces is quite powerful and arresting, it seems to me. You may be quite right in seeing your suffering as a process of rebirth. There is another insight you might consider to add to that idea. The suffering of an enlightened person could be vicarious. Like Christ, you could be sharing the redemptive work of his passion and death by suffering for others, to balance your personal growth with the healing of all the rest of humanity. Your perspective will keep broadening and deepening as you continue the birthing process into eternal life. You quote of Gal. 2:20 suggests that you probably already have this intuition. It will get clearer.

In Christ's love,

(signature)
Thomas Keating

SAINT BENEDICT'S MONASTERY
CISTERCIAN monks

February 13, 2016

Marie Gunderson
P.O. Box 5382
East Lismore
NSW 2480
AUSTRALIA

Dear Marie,

You are welcome to use parts from my letters as you may wish. I am glad you are getting local encouragement. I hope your cancer treatment continues to go well. You are indeed blest to feel completely calm in the situation.

In Christ's love,

Thomas Keating

Appendix B

"St. John of the Cross and the Dark Night of the Soul" by Marie Gundersen

I am writing this article to help clarify the difference between depression and the 'Dark Night of the Soul.' I am also attempting to give readers a brief introduction to the stages of spiritual transformation described by St. John of the Cross in his writing. St. John of the Cross (Juan de Yepes) was a sixteenth-century Spanish mystic, poet and Doctor of the church.

I have noticed that the expression the 'Dark Night of the Soul' is often used incorrectly to describe an emotional/mental experience of depression. However, the term the 'Dark Night of the Soul' originated from St. John of the Cross's poem 'The Dark Night' and depicts the soul's spiritual journey through a process of purification to union with God. The stanzas of this poem are expounded on and include commentaries in the book *Dark Night of The Soul*.

Generally speaking, a person who suffers from depression is often excessively self-concerned and introspective, lacking hope and interest in life. Various therapies and lifestyle changes can lift the person's mood and sometimes medication will be necessary. Usually they can then re-engage in worldly pursuits and social interaction with enthusiasm. The Dark Night of the Soul, however, cannot be addressed psychologically or medically. Depression and deep suffering through loss can accompany the Dark Night of the Soul. St. John acknowledges this overlap. Nevertheless depression and the Dark Night differ both in their cause and in the way that they affect the individual. The cause of the Dark Night is spiritual and in and of itself it produces love, humility, patience and other virtues.

A person entering the Dark Night would have had an experience of Divine Love followed by the loss of this connection. It is this loss that creates a deep feeling of aloneness and a longing for that which is beyond what gives temporary satisfaction. St. John of the Cross says: ...*nothing worldly satisfies one who has tasted the Divine.** This is not a psychological need but a spiritual need. The only resolution to the Dark Night of the Soul is to have faith and to accept that it is a transformative process necessary for union with the Beloved.

The purpose of the Dark Night is to empty the soul of its worldly desires and attachments so that the light of God (the Holy Spirit) can illuminate it. St. John of the Cross insists, along with scriptures, that any attachment to finite things is an impurity that prevents the complete union with God who is infinite love—for union with God can only be a union in likeness.

> *To understand the nature of this union, one should first know that God sustains every soul and dwells in it substantially. ... Consequently, in discussing union with God we are not discussing the substantial union that always exists, but the soul's union with and transformation in God that does not always exist, except when there is likeness of love.*

St. John of the Cross also writes: *...the favour of the world will leave her, and she will lose friends, credit, reputation and even property. ... she must be able to bear the renunciation forever of the satisfactions and delights of the world, and of all worldly comforts. ... the tongues of men will rise up against her and will mock her ... and will set her at nought. Such God sends to those who He will raise to high perfection by proving and refining them as gold in the fire.*

St. John refers to the light of God as the 'Divine Flame of Love,' which he says burns away (purges) faults and produces virtues such as humility and compassion. He reminds us that: *he that humbles himself is exalted and he that exalts himself is humbled.* (To be humbled is not the same as experiencing low self-esteem, when it is necessary to restore a healthier self-image.)

St. John uses the metaphor of the dark night to signify the ending of satisfaction and gratification in worldly things—this is like a deprivation or 'night' to the senses and the emotions. In some mysterious way the affective mechanism is 'put to sleep' leaving the person 'in darkness,' not knowing what is happening. Without the usual emotional feedback the person is left feeling empty and in a void, where all seems dry and lifeless.

Closer to union with God the process of purification intensifies, just as in relation to night it is always darkest before dawn. St. John also uses the metaphor of darkness to imply that the infusion of spiritual light cannot be perceived by the senses or the intellect. (The Spanish word for dark is *oscura* and means obscure.)

The pathway taken for the journey through the Dark Night of the Soul is portrayed as a secret staircase (secret because it is unknown to the intellect). St. John writes about ten steps that are necessary for the soul to ascend in order to reach union with God. The final step can only be perfected in the afterlife. The soul is elevated step by step, gradually relinquishing egocentric ways and surrendering to God.

The metaphor of the staircase is also used to show how the soul does not remain in one state for long, but continuously ascends and descends this ladder of love. There will be a fluctuation of highs and lows until the soul reaches a state of tranquillity and peace, united in Love with the Beloved. Union with God is not a fixed state, but it continues to deepen.

In his writings St. John of the Cross describes two different nights (stages): the 'Dark Night of Sense' followed by the 'Dark Night of Spirit.' During the Night of Sense we are purged of the desires and attachments experienced through the senses. The intellect too will be purged (made empty) of its conditioning (concepts and opinions) in order to receive the illumination of God's wisdom; for God exceeds all understanding and knowledge. And the personal will needs to be renounced to God's eternal will: 'Not my will, but Thy will.'

In the Night of Spirit there are further purifications, more on a mental and spiritual level as the inflow of light intensifies. Impurities not seen as clearly before are highlighted and purged. Attitudes and presumptions, old habits and patterns of behaviour are now exposed because they are in contrast to the presence of Divine Light. All that is impure and unholy is purged by this Divine flame of love. This is a time to surrender and let the Holy Spirit do the work.

There is also an increasing yearning for a permanent union with God: *It is observed that the absence of the Beloved is a continual sighing in the heart of the lover because apart from Him she loves nought, rests in nought and finds relief in nought.*

There are two aspects to each Night: an 'active night' and a 'passive night.' These do not operate separately; they are both part of the process and one is dependent on the other.

The 'active night' refers to what *we* can do, such as work on ourselves (make conscious our shadow side), live virtuously, practise meditation and pray. St. John of the Cross writes: *An act of virtue produces and fosters in the soul: mildness, peace, comfort, light, purity and strength.*

St. John's use of the word 'meditation' implies 'to reflect on' by using one's intellect or imagination. Meditation leads to contemplation, which is the term he uses for being present to what is (open awareness). Being attentive to every moment of life will lead to greater awareness; observing one's thoughts, feelings and actions increases self-knowledge. St. John makes it clear that self-knowledge is essential for transformation.

When the mind is silent (in contemplative prayer), free of images and chatter, we will be more receptive to the Divine presence: 'Be still and know that I am God.' (Psalm 46)

During the 'passive night' it is the Light of God (Holy Spirit) rather than one's own efforts that accomplishes the purification. The Holy Spirit elevates the soul from time to time during the purgation and refreshes the soul by relieving it of the agony of annihilation.

The completion of this purification (the Night of Spirit) is not abrupt, rather there is a gradual dissolution of the feeling of aloneness which is being extinguished by the inflow of Divine Light and Love. St. John of the Cross writes: *The heart that is wounded with the pain of Thy absence will be healed with the delight and glory of Thy sweet presence.*

In union with God the person abides in a sublime state of peace and tranquillity. This is how St. John of the Cross expressed it in the last stanza of his poem 'Dark Night':

I abandoned and forgot myself,
laying my face on my Beloved;
all things ceased; I went out from myself,
leaving my cares forgotten among the lilies.

*All quotes come from 'The Collected Works of St. John of the Cross.' Translated by Kieran Kavanaugh and Otilio Rodriguez. ICS Publications, Institute of Carmelite Studies, Washington DC, 1991.

'Dark Night' by St. John of the Cross

1. On a dark night, Kindled in love with yearnings—oh, happy chance!—
I went forth without being observed, My house being now at rest.

2. In darkness and secure, By the secret ladder, disguised—oh, happy chance!—
In darkness and in concealment, My house being now at rest.

3. In the happy night, In secret, when none saw me,
Nor I beheld aught, Without light or guide, save that which burned in my heart.

4. This light guided me More surely than the light of noonday
To the place where he (well I knew who!) was awaiting me—

A place where none appeared.

5. Oh, night that guided me, Oh, night more lovely than the dawn,
Oh, night that joined Beloved with lover, Lover transformed in the Beloved!

6. Upon my flowery breast, Kept wholly for himself alone,
There he stayed sleeping, and I caressed him, And the fanning of the cedars made a breeze.

7. The breeze blew from the turret As I parted his locks;
With his gentle hand he wounded my neck And caused all my senses to be suspended.

8. I remained, lost in oblivion; My face I reclined on the Beloved.
All ceased and I abandoned myself, Leaving my cares forgotten among the lilies. \

From *The Complete Works of Saint John of the Cross*. Translated and edited by E. Allison Peers. Robert MacLehose & Co. Ltd., 1935.

Timeline of Mystical Experiences

NORWAY

1973 (Aug.) Man in lift. Seven floors. (pp. 5)

1975 (Feb.) Walking home alone on path across snowfields. (p. 7)

1975 (May) Mystical calling while stepping across threshold. (p. 8)

1976 (Feb.) Bicycling home with Patrick. Seeing a vision of a cross in the sky. (p. 8)

AUSTRALIA

1978 (April) While talking about Man in the lift, sudden gust of wind. (p. 11)

1980 (Nov.) Spiritual being touching my big toe. (p. 13)

1981 (March) Three mysterious calls of a bird. (pp. 13)

1981 (May) Out-of-body experience. Learning thoughts affect force. (p. 14)

1981 (June) Out-of-body experience. EMAD—'killing' the dragon. (p. 15)

1982 (April) Three mysterious knocks on the front door. (p. 20)

1987 (Aug.) Inner voice announcing: 'You will be turned inside out.' (p. 22)

1990 (June) Mysteriously drops of water fall into our open eyes. (pp. 24)

1990 (Aug.) Drops Paul. Message to me: 'It is your turn now.' (p. 26)

1990 (24 Oct.) Force enters making me feel like an empty vessel. (pp. 27)

1993 (July) Inner voice: 'You are eligible for a demonstration.' (p. 31)

1997 Making appointment with hypnotherapist. Three mysterious knocks on the door. (p. 36)

1999 (17 Dec.) Force ascending. (p. 45)

2001 (11 Sept.) Witness two birds crash into two tall windows at home. (p. 49)

2003 (Nov.) I am 'made' to write my name as 'Mary.' (p. 56)

2007 Unintentional capitalisation of the words 'FROM THE GROUND FLOOR TO THE SEVENTH FLOOR.' (p. 69)

2012 (Feb.) Divine inner light turned off. (p. 78)

2015 (May) Inner vision of grotto. (p. 84)

2017 (Sept.) Inner vision of tree on the hill. (p. 87)

2019 Sentence in red, in Reflections on the Journey. (p. 111)

Selected Bibliography

Aurobindo, Sri. *Letters on Yoga, Vol. II*. Pondicherry, India: Sri Aurobindo Ashram Press, 1958.
Bourgeault, Cynthia. *The Heart of Centering Prayer*. Boulder, CO: Shambhala Publications, 2016.
Douglas-Klotz, Neil. *Prayers of the Cosmos*. New York: Harper San Francisco, 1990.
Dürckheim, Karlfried G. *The Way of Transformation*. London: Allen and Unwin, 1971.
Evans, Patricia. *The Verbally Abusive Relationship*. Avon, MA: Adams Media, 1992.
Gaffney, Mark. H. *Gnostic Secrets of the Naassenes*. Rochester, NY: Inner Traditions, 2004.
Greenwell, Bonnie. *Energies of Transformation*. Saratoga, CA: Shakti River Press, 1990.
Griffiths, Bede. *Universal Wisdom*. London: Fount, 1994.
Grof, Christina and Stanislav Grof. *The Stormy Search for the Self*. London: Mandala, 1991.
Keating, Thomas. *Invitation to Love: The Way of Christian Contemplation*. New York, London: Continuum, 1992.
———. *The Better Part: Stages of Contemplative Living*. New York: Continuum, 2007.

Kempis, Thomas à. *The Imitation of Christ.* London: The Whitefriars Press Ltd., 1952.

Khan, Hidayat Inayat. *Sufi Teaching: Lectures from Lake O'Hara.* Victoria, BC: Ekstasis Editions, 1994.

Kornfield, Jack. *A Path with Heart.* New York: Bantam Books, 1993.

Krishna, Gopi. *Kundalini: The Evolutionary Energy in Man.* Berkeley, CA: Shambhala Publications, 1970.

———. *Living with Kundalini: The Autobiography of Gopi Krishna.* Boston: Shambhala Publications, 1993.

Krishnamurti, Jiddu. *Freedom from the Known.* New York: HarperSanFrancisco, 1969.

———. *Krishnamurti on Education.* New Delhi: Orient Longman Ltd., 1974.

Lawrence, D. H. 'Phoenix.' *Emergence* 5 (2001).

Lievegoed, Bernard. *Man on the Threshold.* Stroud, UK: Hawthorn Press, 1983.

Lutyens, Mary. *Krishnamurti: The Years of Awakening.* London: John Murray Ltd., 1975.

———. *Krishnamurti: The Open Door.* London: John Murray Ltd., 1988.

Miller, Robert. J. *The Complete Gospels.* Santa Rosa, CA: Polebridge Press, 1994.

Peers, E. Allison. *The Complete Works of Saint John of the Cross.* Wheathampstead, UK: Anthony Clarke, 1935.

———. *Dark Night of the Soul by St. John of the Cross.* New York: Doubleday, 1959.

Roberts, Bernadette. *The Path to No-Self.* Boston: Shambhala Publications, 1985.

Sananda, Solomae. *Kundalini and the Evolution of Consciousness.* Inola, OK: Living Spirit Press, 2003.

Strobel, Lee. *The Case for Christ.* Grand Rapids, MI: Zondervan, 1998.

Suzuki, D.T. *The Zen Doctrine of No Mind.* London: Rider and Company, 1949.

Underhill, Evelyn. *Mysticism.* London: Bracken Books, 1942.

U Pandita, Sayadaw. *In This Very Life.* Boston: Wisdom Publications, 1992.

Wei, Wei Wu. *Ask the Awakened.* Boulder, CO: Sentient Publications, 2002.